hamlyn

# soups

Ingeborg Pertwee

## Notes

Both metric and imperial measurements have been given in all recipes.
Use one set of measurements only and not a mixture of both.
Standard level spoon measurements are used in all recipes.
1 tablespoon = one 15 ml spoon
1 teaspoon = one 5 ml spoon
Eggs should be medium unless otherwise stated.
Milk should be full fat unless otherwise stated.
Pepper should be freshly ground black pepper unless otherwise stated.
Fresh herbs should be used unless otherwise stated. If unavailable
use dried herbs as an alternative but halve the quantities stated.

## Acknowledgements

Art Editor Mark Winwood
Designer Leigh Jones
Commissioning Editor Nicky Hill
Editor Sasha Judelson
Editorial Assistant Kathy Steer
Production Controller Melanie Frantz
Photographer Diana Miller
Home Economist Louise Pickford
Stylist Wei Tang

First published in Great Britain in 1996 by Hamlyn
a division of Octopus Publishing Group Limited
2–4 Heron Quays, London E14 4JP

This paperback edition first published in 2001

ISBN 0 600 60545 0

A CIP catalogue record for this book is available from the British Library
Produced by Toppan, Hong Kong
Printed in China

sdnos

# Contents

# Soup, glorious soup!

There are few dishes as versatile as soup:
the choice of ingredients is vast,
the variations limitless. Soup can be
prepared out of almost anything
and there is scarcely an occasion when
a bowl of soup is not welcome, whether
as a warming first course to a
dinner, a hearty one-dish supper or
a refreshing, chilled starter for a
summer's lunch.

A gloomy winter's day appears less chilly when a steaming bowl of soup is on the table, and an autumn picnic will be enlivened by a flask of nourishing, hearty minestrone or lentil soup. Economy must also be added to its list of virtues, because by using seasonal produce soup is an inexpensive dish which, perhaps, explains its humble origin.

The French word 'soupe' is used to describe not just a liquid preparation but various ingredients added to a broth. It is also the derivation of the word 'supper'. When the humble soup was finally accepted into the dining rooms of the middle and upper classes it had been transformed into a much more sophisticated dish which was rather confusingly categorized as consommé, bouillon, purée, velouté, crème, bisque, petit marmite or potage. Nowadays some of this complicated labelling has been discarded in everyday use, and there are basically four kinds of soup: stock, broth, thickened soup and purée.

## Stocks

Meal and Poultry Stock is either made from raw bones or leftovers with a few added vegetables, herbs and spices.

Fish Stock is the most economic and easiest to make. It can be prepared from a great variety of fresh vegetables.

Broth is unclarified and mostly served with meat, poultry and game in which it was prepared. Usually the only added ingredients are rice, barley and diced vegetables.

Thickened Soups can be made from meat, poultry, fish or vegetables and are thickened with flour, cornflour, arrowroot and sometimes a combination of eggs and cream.

Pureé is perhaps the healthiest, most popular and also the simplest kind of soup to make. But a liquidizer or food processor is vital – the latter being more useful as its capacity is usually larger and the engine more powerful.

A pureéd soup can be made of almost any vegetable and its thickness is caused by blending the ingredients of which it is composed. Potatoes in particular help to make the pureé smooth and even. Meat, poultry, game, fish or shellfish may be added later.

## The Alternative to Homemade Stock

There is no doubt that good homemade stock is an important ingredient of any soup. But unfortunately stock-making is a time-consuming procedure that needs to be planned well in advance.

For those who are too busy to make their own, there is a huge variety of excellent stock cubes available from shops and supermarkets.

Some major branches of supermarkets sell containers of fresh meat, poultry and fish stock which have an authentic homemade flavour.

Major health food shops stock good instant substitutes which are salt-reduced, free of artificial flavour enhancers, glucose and lactose, as well as all types of artificial colouring and preservatives.

## Garnishing Soups

When serving a soup it is important to give attention to its appearance.

A bowl of pallid liquid is visually unappealing, no matter how delicious it may taste. All soups – even the modest ones – can be made to look special with the simplest additions.

A sprinkling of chopped green herbs embellishes a colourless soup; toasted pine nuts or flaked almonds give a contrast of texture to creamy soups or, if taking into account the main ingredient, garnish a pureé made from broccoli or cauliflower with tiny blanched florets, an asparagus soup with one or two cooked asparagus tips, or scatter a few peas over the surface of a smooth pea soup.

A swirl of single or soured cream or – for the more artistic cook – a feathery pattern of cream drawn across the top, enhances a darker soup.

There are countless ways to dress up a soup; all you need is imagination and a few handy tips.

## Soup Garnishes

### Almonds

Blanched and toasted then chopped, almonds give a pleasant crunch to cream and fruit soups.

### Basil

Used sparingly, snipped fresh basil leaves add a pleasant flavour to tomato, cucumber and some fish soups.

### Cheese

Grated Parmesan, Gruyère or Cheddar can be served separately or sprinkled on top of some vegetable soups, especially Minestrone and Onion Soup, Broccoli Soup and Aubergine Soup.

## Chervil

Similar to parsley in flavour but milder, this delicate herb can be snipped and sprinkled over most soups especially fish and shellfish, poultry and vegetable soups.

## Chives

A necessary garnish for 'Vichyssoise', but snipped chives go well with a great number of soups, like cucumber, avocado, asparagus, tomato, potato and some fish soups.

## Coriander

Also known as 'Chinese parsley' coriander has a fresh taste, a little similar to orange. Chop it finely and scatter it over carrot, parsnip, turnip and potato soups.

## Croûtons

Make these by frying 5 mm/¼ inch diced brown or white bread in olive oil until golden brown and crisp all over.

For garlic flavoured croûtons add 2 peeled and halved garlic cloves to the oil. Drain the croûtons on absorbent kitchen paper. (See page 66.)

Croûtons add an extra crunch to most chowders, some vegetable soups and puréed soups.

## Crumbled Bacon

Fry or grill lean rashers of bacon until very crisp. Drain them thoroughly on absorbent kitchen paper and when cold crumble or crush them. Crumbled or crushed bacon enhances the flavour of vegetable, potato, lentil and pea soups.

## Dill

A delicately flavoured herb with a very slight caraway flavour. It goes well with cucumber, artichoke and most fish soups including Cream of Smoked Salmon Soup.

## Fennel

This feathery herb looks like dill but is entirely different in taste and its snipped leaves are a suitable garnish for fish and shellfish soups.

## Mint

There are many varieties of mint grown, but from the cook's point of view only two are of importance. Finely chopped apple mint is delicious on all types of chilled fruit soups, but generally the ordinary garden mint is best on pea, potato and other vegetable soups.

## Onion

Very finely grated, mild onion can be used sparingly on some vegetable soups.

## Orange Rind

A little shredded and blanched orange rind can be placed gently on some carrot-based and also shellfish soups.

## Paprika

A dusting of rich red paprika adds striking colour to pale creamy chowders and soups, especially Potato Chowder and Celeriac and Apple Soup.

## Parsley

The most popular of all garnishes. Finely chopped it can be scattered over all but fruit soups.

The two common varieties are the flat-leaved and curly-leaved parsley.

## Pine Nuts

A few pine nuts toasted under the grill go well on spinach, cabbage, cauliflower or Jerusalem artichoke soups.

## Spring Onions

The top green part of spring onions, when finely chopped, can be used as a substitute for chives. Spring onions are also excellent on chilled soups and also tomato, cucumber, potato, vegetable or curry soups.

## Tomato

Skinned, deseeded and finely chopped tomatoes are a suitable garnish for cold soups, such as Gazpacho.

Skin the tomatoes by making a small cross in the top of the tomatoes then place in a bowl and pour boiling water over them and leave to stand for 1 minute. Remove with a slotted spoon and allow to cool. Carefully slip off the skins with a sharp pointed knife.

## Walnuts

A few finely chopped walnuts give a crunchy texture to most puréed soups.

## Watercress

The slightly peppery taste of finely chopped watercress leaves can be used sparingly on chowders, cream and other fish soups.

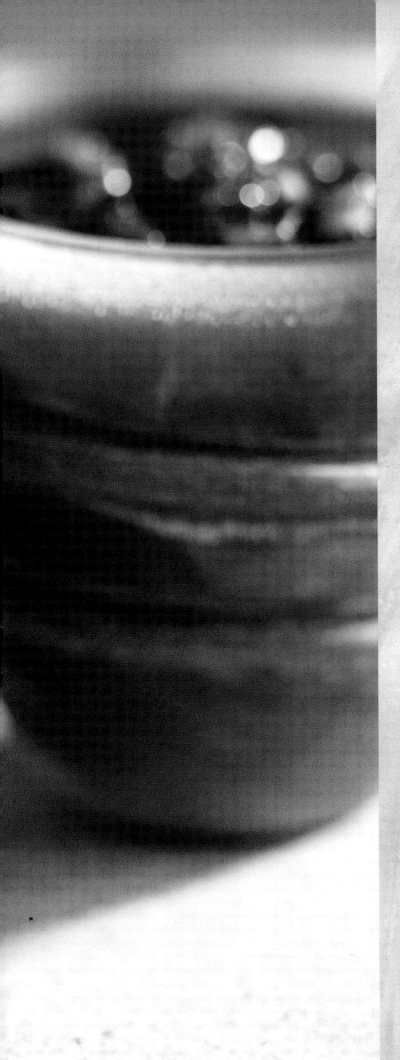

# Summer Soups

This chapter contains some wonderfully refreshing cold soups which make ideal starters for hot sunny days. If serving a cold soup, for best results make sure that the soup bowls or plates are very well chilled before adding the really cold soup. It is well worth rembering that many chilled soups are also delicious served hot if the weather suddenly changes.

(Most of the recipes are quick and easy to prepare and make use of vegetables in season.)

# Chilled Watercress Soup

Watercress is pleasantly pungent and gives this soup an almost peppery flavour and is illustrated on pages 10–11.

**I** Melt the butter or margarine in a saucepan. Cook the watercress over a moderate heat for 3 minutes, stirring frequently. Add the stock, potatoes and nutmeg with pepper to taste. Bring to the boil, then lower the heat and simmer, covered, for 15–20 minutes, or until the potatoes are soft. Leave to cool.
**2** In a blender or food processor purée the mixture in batches until smooth, transferring each successive batch, to a large bowl. Cover closely and chill in the refrigerator for at least 3 hours.
**3** Just before serving, fold in the chilled cream. Add salt if necessary. Serve in chilled bowls, garnishing each portion with a few watercress leaves, and a little oil and black pepper, if using.

*50 g/2 oz butter or margarine*

*2 bunches of watercress, thick stems discarded, chopped coarsely*

*I litre/1¾ pints Chicken or Vegetable stock (see page 122)*

*250 g/8 oz potatoes, peeled and chopped*

*pinch of grated nutmeg*

*salt and pepper*

*To garnish:*

*150 ml/¼ pint single cream, chilled*

*a few watercress leaves*

*I tablespoon olive oil (optional)*

- Serves 4–6
- Preparation time: about 10 minutes, plus 3 hours chilling time
- Cooking time: 25 minutes

*Variation*

## Watercress and Apple Soup

**I** Melt the butter or margarine in a saucepan. Add the watercress and apples and cook for 3–5 minutes over a moderate heat. Stir frequently. Add the stock, potatoes, lemon juice and nutmeg, with salt and pepper to taste. Bring to the boil, then lower the heat and simmer, covered, for 15–20 minutes, or until the apples and potatoes are soft.
**2** In a blender or food processor purée the mixture in batches until smooth, transferring each successive batch to a clean saucepan. Add the cream and gently reheat without boiling. Serve in heated soup bowls or plates. Sprinkle each portion with some of the finely chopped apple to garnish.

*50 g/2 oz butter or margarine*

*2 bunches of watercress, thick stems discarded, chopped coarsely*

*125 g/4 oz peeled, cored and chopped dessert apples*

*I litre/1¾ pints Chicken or Vegetable Stock (see page 122)*

*250 g/8 oz potatoes, peeled and chopped*

*I teaspoon lemon juice*

*pinch of grated nutmeg*

*150 ml/¼ pint single cream, chilled*

*salt and pepper*

*I tablespoon finely chopped dessert apple, to garnish*

- Serves 4–6
- Preparation time: 15 minutes
- Cooking time: 25–30 minutes

# Chilled Lettuce and Dill Soup

The coarse, outer leaves of the lettuce give this soup its interesting flavour, while the hearts can be kept for a salad.

**I** Melt the butter or margarine in a saucepan. Add the onion, and cook, stirring occasionally, over a moderate heat until soft. Add the flour and cook, stirring, for 2 minutes more. Whisk in the stock. Bring to the boil, whisking constantly.

**2** Add the shredded lettuce, 2 tablespoons of the snipped dill and the nutmeg. Lower the heat and simmer, uncovered, for about 15 minutes, stirring occasionally. Leave to cool.

**3** In a blender or food processor purée the mixture in batches until smooth. Transfer each successive batch to a bowl. Stir in the lemon juice and pepper, with salt to taste. Cover closely and chill in the refrigerator for at least 3 hours.

**4** In a small bowl mix the remaining dill with the cream. Serve the soup in chilled bowls, garnishing each portion with a swirl of the cream and dill mixture.

*50 g/2 oz butter or margarine*

*I small onion, chopped*

*I tablespoon plain flour*

*900 ml/1½ pints Chicken or Vegetable Stock (see page 122)*

*the outer leaves of 2 round lettuces, coarsely shredded*

*3 tablespoons snipped fresh dill*

*pinch of grated nutmeg*

*I tablespoon lemon juice*

*¼–½ teaspoon ground white pepper*

*salt*

*4 tablespoons double cream*

- Serves 4
- Preparation time: 10 minutes, plus 3 hours chilling time
- Cooking time: about 20 minutes

# Cream of Asparagus Soup

**I** Trim the ends of the asparagus, and cut into 1 inch/2.5 cm segments. In a large saucepan bring 2 litres/3½ pints of lightly salted water to the boil, add the asparagus and cook, until very tender. Drain, reserving the stock in a jug.

**2** Melt the butter in a heavy-bottomed saucepan, stir in the flour and cook for 1 minute. Gradually add the asparagus stock, stirring constantly until the mixture boils and thickens. Add the nutmeg, with salt and white pepper to taste. Cook for 3–5 minutes, stirring frequently.

**3** Add the asparagus segments and lower the heat. Cook for a further 5 minutes, stirring from time to time.

**4** In a small bowl beat the egg yolks with the cream, add a little more pepper and pour the mixture into the soup. Stir well and cook for 1 minute more without boiling. Serve in heated soup plates or bowls, garnishing each portion with a sprinkling of snipped chives.

*I kg/2 lb asparagus*

*25 g/I oz butter*

*I tablespoon plain flour*

*pinch of grated nutmeg*

*2 egg yolks*

*300 ml/½ pint double cream*

*salt and white pepper*

*I tablespoon snipped fresh chives, to garnish*

- Serves 6
- Preparation time: 10 minutes
- Cooking time: about 30 minutes

13

# Cold Curried Chicken Soup

Served with French bread this spicy soup is a perfect starter to a light lunch on a hot summer's day. All that is required to complete the meal is a salad.

**1** Bring 1 litre/1¾ pints of the stock to the boil in a saucepan. Add the chicken breast, reduce the heat to the lowest setting and simmer, covered, for 8–10 minutes, turning the chicken breast once. Using tongs or a slotted spoon remove the chicken and chop it finely on a board. Reserve the remaining hot stock in a jug.

**2** Melt the butter or margarine in a separate saucepan. Add the celery, onion and apple, and cook covered, for 10–12 minutes over a moderate heat. Stir from time to time. Add the curry powder and cook for 2 minutes more, stirring all the time. Stir in the flour and cook for 1 minute, then pour in the remaining 450 ml/¾ pint stock and stir well. Bring the mixture to the boil, lower the heat and simmer for 10 minutes, stirring occasionally.

**3** In a blender or food processor purée the mixture until smooth. Transfer it to a bowl. Stir in the chutney, the reserved chicken stock in the jug and the chopped chicken breast. When cool, cover the soup closely and chill for at least 3 hours.

*1.25 litres/2½ pints Chicken Stock (see page 122)*

*1 boneless, skinless chicken breast, halved*

*50 g/2 oz butter or margarine*

*1 celery stick, sliced*

*1 onion, chopped*

*1 dessert apple, peeled, cored and chopped*

*2 tablespoons medium hot curry powder*

*2 tablespoons plain flour*

*1 tablespoon chutney*

- Serves 6
- Preparation time: 15 minutes, plus 3 hours chilling time
- Cooking time: about 35 minutes

# Chilled Potato Chowder

This delicious chowder is illustrated opposite.

**1** Place the potatoes and onions in a saucepan. Add just enough water to cover and cook the vegetables until tender. Drain and rub the mixture through a coarse sieve into a clean pan.

**2** Add the mushroom soup, butter or margarine, milk and mustard, with salt and pepper to taste. Stir well. Heat gently until the soup begins to simmer. Pour the soup into a bowl and leave to cool.

**3** Cover the bowl closely and chill the chowder in the refrigerator for at least 3 hours.

**4** Serve the soup in chilled bowls, garnishing each portion with a little cottage cheese, a few snipped chives and a dusting of paprika.

*5 potatoes, peeled and diced*

*3 onions, sliced*

*1 x 475 g/15 oz can cream of mushroom soup*

*25 g/1 oz butter or margarine*

*900 ml/1½ pints milk*

*1 teaspoon prepared English mustard*

*salt and pepper*

*To garnish:*

*2 tablespoons cottage cheese*

*a few snipped chives*

*paprika*

- Serves 6
- Preparation time: 10 minutes, plus 3 hours chilling time
- Cooking time: about 20 minutes

**14**

# Jellied Beetroot Soup

**1** Grate the beetroot into a large bowl.

**2** Place the onions, carrots, parsley, peppercorns and bay leaf in a pan. Add 1 litre/1¾ pints water and bring to the boil. Lower the heat, cover and simmer for 1 hour or until all the vegetables are soft and have flavoured the stock.

**3** Pour the stock through a large strainer into the bowl containing the beetroot; mix well. Discard the contents of the strainer. Return the beetroot and stock to the clean pan. Add the sugar and vinegar, with salt to taste. Simmer for 10 minutes. Do not allow to boil. Strain into a clean pan discarding the beetroot.

**4** Spoon 2 tablespoons of the hot soup into a cup. Stir in the gelatine until thoroughly dissolved, then return the mixture to the remaining soup, stirring well. Set aside. When cold, pour it into a bowl, cover closely and chill in the refrigerator for at least 3 hours, or until set. Just before serving break up the jellied soup and serve in chilled bowls. Spoon the soured cream into a small bowl. Stir in the curry powder. Garnish with the soured cream mixture, sprinkled with chives.

- Serves 4–6
- Preparation time: about 20 minutes, plus 3 hours chilling time
- Cooking time: 1¼ hours

*4 peeled cooked beetroot*

*2 onions, chopped*

*2 carrots, chopped*

*3 sprigs of parsley*

*6 black peppercorns*

*1 bay leaf*

*1 sugar cube or 1 teaspoon of sugar*

*2 teaspoons white wine vinegar*

*1½ teaspoons powdered gelatine*

*salt*

*To garnish:*

*150 ml/¼ pint soured cream*

*1 teaspoon mild curry powder*

*snipped fresh chives*

## Variation

# Chilled Beetroot Soup

Follow the main recipe up to step 3 but strain the soup into a large bowl. Cover closely and chill in the refrigerator for at least 3 hours. Serve the soup in chilled bowls, garnished with soured cream.

- Serves 4–6
- Preparation time: about 20 minutes, plus 3 hours chilling time
- Cooking time: 1½ hours

# Chilled Tomato Soup

Smooth in texture and deliciously refreshing, this soup has all the sweet fruity flavour of tomatoes.

**1** Heat the olive oil and butter in a heavy-bottomed saucepan. Cook the onion and garlic over a moderate heat for 3–5 minutes, or until transparent but not golden. Add the tomatoes and cook for 3 minutes more stirring frequently.

**2** Pour in the chicken stock and add the oregano, caster sugar, celery salt, nutmeg, and the Worcestershire sauce, with salt and pepper to taste. Stir well, bring to the boil, then lower the heat and simmer, partially covered, for 45 minutes. Cool the mixture slightly.

*2 tablespoons olive oil*

*25 g/1 oz butter*

*1 large onion, chopped*

*1 garlic clove, chopped*

*750 g–1 kg/1½ lb–2 lb tomatoes, skinned (see page 9) and chopped coarsely*

*900 ml/1½ pints Chicken Stock (see page 122)*

*1 teaspoon chopped fresh oregano or ½ teaspoon dried oregano*

*1½ teaspoons caster sugar*

*¼ teaspoon celery salt*

*pinch of grated nutmeg*

*1 tablespoon Worcestershire sauce*

*150 ml/¼ pint soured cream*

*salt and pepper*

*To garnish:*

*6 Spanish olives*

*chopped fresh parsley*

**3** In a blender or food processor purée the mixture in batches transferring each successive batch to a bowl. Stir in the soured cream and allow the soup to cool completely, then cover the bowl closely and chill it in the refrigerator for at least 3 hours.

**4** Meanwhile place a Spanish olive in each section of a 6-cube ice tray and top with cold water. Freeze until solid. Serve the soup in chilled bowls, with an olive-filled ice cube on each serving. Add a sprinkling of parsley to each portion.

- Serves 6
- Preparation time: about 20 minutes, plus 3 hours chilling time
- Cooking time: 50–55 minutes

**17**

# Gazpacho

This, Spain's most famous soup, is the ultimate starter during the hot summer months. Served ice cold in chilled bowls, as seen opposite, it is refreshing and tangy.

**1** Combine the chopped garlic and salt in a mortar and pound with a pestle until it is smooth. Alternatively place the garlic and salt on a board and crush the garlic with the flattened blade of a knife. Place the bread in a bowl covered with cold water. Soak for 5 seconds, then drain the bread, squeezing out the moisture.

**2** Set aside a quarter of the tomatoes, onions, cucumber and peppers for the garnish. Place the remaining vegetables in a blender or food processor. Add the garlic paste, bread and oil and purée the mixture until it is very smooth.

*2 garlic cloves, chopped roughly*

*¼ teaspoon salt*

*3 slices of thick white bread, crusts removed*

*1 kg/2 lb tomatoes, skinned (see page 9) and chopped coarsely*

*2 onions, coarsely chopped*

*½ large cucumber, peeled, deseeded and chopped coarsely*

*2 large green peppers, cored, deseeded and chopped coarsely*

*5 tablespoons olive oil*

*4 tablespoons white wine vinegar*

*freshly ground black pepper*

**3** Pour the mixture into a bowl and stir in the vinegar and 1 litre/1¾ pints water with pepper to taste. Cover closely and chill in the refrigerator for at least 3 hours.

**4** Chop the reserved vegetables very finely and serve them separately in small bowls with the soup. Serve the soup very cold in individual chilled bowls. Each guest adds a selection of the vegetable accompaniments to his or her portion, as liked. Croûtons (see page 66) may also be offered.

- Serves 6
- Preparation time: 10–15 minutes, plus
  3 hours chilling time

*Variation*

# Spicy Gazpacho with Prawns

Follow the main recipe but add ½ teaspoon each of Tabasco sauce, Worcestershire sauce and ground cumin when purée-ing the mixture in the blender or food processor. Stir in 275 g/9 oz cooked peeled prawns with the vinegar, the measured water and the black pepper. Proceed as in the main recipe.

*½ teaspoon Tabasco sauce*

*½ teaspoon Worcestershire sauce*

*½ teaspoon ground cumin*

*275 g/9 oz cooked and peeled prawns (thawed if frozen)*

- Serves 6
- Preparation time:
  10–15 minutes, plus
  3 hours chilling time

*Variation*

# Chilled 'Bloody Mary' Gazpacho

This variation of Gazpacho, illustrated on pages 10–11, is ideal for a starter at a barbecue or picnic. After chilling the soup transfer it to a vacuum flask if you are planning a picnic.

**1** In a bowl whisk together the vinegar, lemon juice, tomato juice, celery salt, Tabasco and Worcestershire sauce. Add salt and pepper to taste and whisk in the vodka, if using.

**2** In a slow stream pour in the oil, then add the tomatoes, cucumber, peppers and onion. Cover the bowl closely and chill in the refrigerator for at least 3 hours.

- Serves 4
- Preparation time: 10 minutes, plus 3 hours chilling time

*1½ tablespoons white wine vinegar*

*1 tablespoon fresh lemon juice*

*600 ml/1 pint tomato juice, chilled*

*¼ teaspoon celery salt*

*¼ teaspoon Tabasco sauce, or to taste*

*1 teaspoon Worcestershire sauce*

*2 tablespoons vodka (optional)*

*2 tablespoons olive oil*

*4 tomatoes, skinned (see page 9), chopped and deseeded*

*½ large cucumber, peeled, deseeded and finely chopped*

*2 green peppers, cored, deseeded and finely chopped*

*1 onion, finely chopped*

*salt and ground black pepper*

# Vichyssoise

This sophisticated iced soup is made from humble ingredients: leeks and potatoes. It can be prepared 24 hours in advance and must be velvety smooth and well chilled.

**I** Slice off the green tops of the leeks and set aside for use in another recipe. Slice the white parts of the leeks thinly.

**2** Melt the butter or margarine in a pan. Add the leeks and onion and cook over a moderate heat for 5 minutes, stirring constantly. Do not allow the vegetables to change colour.

**3** Add the stock, nutmeg and potatoes with salt and pepper to taste. Bring the mixture to the boil, lower the heat and cook, partially covered, for 25 minutes. Pour in the milk and simmer for 5-8 minutes more. Cool slightly.

**4** In a blender or food processor purée the mixture in batches until smooth, then rub it through a sieve into a bowl. Add the single cream, stir well and cover the bowl closely. Chill in the refrigerator for at least 3 hours. Just before serving swirl in the double cream and add more salt and pepper if required. Serve in chilled bowls, garnishing each portion with a generous sprinkling of snipped chives.

*I kg/2 lb leeks, trimmed and cleaned*

*50 g/2 oz butter or margarine*

*I onion, chopped*

*I litre/1¾ pints Chicken or Vegetable Stock (see page 122)*

*pinch of grated nutmeg*

*750 g/1½ lb old potatoes, peeled and cubed*

*600 ml/1 pint milk*

*300 ml/½ pint single cream*

*150 ml/¼ pint double cream, chilled*

*salt and white pepper*

*2 tablespoons snipped fresh chives*

- Serves 6
- Preparation time: 15 minutes, plus 3 hours chilling time
- Cooking time: about 35 minutes

## Variation

# *Prawn Vichyssoise*

Follow the main recipe up to step 4. Then add 175 g/6 oz cooked peeled prawns to the soup as instructed in the main recipe. Serve in chilled bowls, garnished with a few prawns.

- Serves 6
- Preparation time: 15 minutes, plus 3 hours chilling time
- Cooking time: about 35 minutes

# Chilled Cucumber and Basil Soup

The cool, delicate flavour of cucumber makes it the ideal ingredient for a variety of refreshing summer soups. Here it is combined with fresh basil to make the delicious soup illustrated opposite.

**1** Melt the butter or margarine in a saucepan. Add the cucumber and cook, covered, for 3–5 minutes or until soft. Stir frequently. Add the stock, potatoes and basil. Bring the mixture to the boil. Cook, partially covered, for 15–20 minutes or until the potatoes are tender. Cool slightly.

**2** In a blender or food processor purée the mixture in batches, transferring each successive batch to a bowl. Add salt and pepper to taste; leave to cool. Cover the bowl closely and chill in the refrigerator for at least 3 hours.

**3** Just before serving, fold the chilled cream into the soup. Serve the soup in chilled bowls and garnish each portion with a basil leaf and a dusting of paprika, if liked.

*50 g/2 oz butter or margarine*

*2 cucumbers, peeled, deseeded and chopped*

*1.2 litres/2 pints Chicken or Vegetable Stock (see page 122)*

*300 g/10 oz potatoes, peeled and chopped*

*2 tablespoons chopped fresh basil leaves*

*150 ml/¼ pint double cream, chilled*

*salt and ground white pepper*

*To garnish:*

*4-6 basil leaves (optional)*

*paprika (optional)*

- Serves 4-6
- Preparation time: 15 minutes, plus 3 hours chilling time
- Cooking time: 20–25 minutes

# Chilled Cucumber Soup with Yogurt and Dill

An ideal combination of flavours which is refreshing and needs no cooking.

**1** Combine the cucumbers and dill with the stock in a blender or food processor; process until very smooth.

**2** Pour the mixture into a bowl and whisk in the yogurt and lemon juice. Add white pepper and salt to taste. Cover closely and refrigerate the soup for at least 3 hours.

**3** Serve the soup in chilled bowls, garnishing each portion with a slice of cucumber and a sprinkling of dill and paprika.

- Serves 4–6
- Preparation time: 10 minutes, plus 3 hours chilling time

*2 cucumbers, peeled deseeded and chopped*

*3 tablespoons snipped fresh dill*

*600 ml/1 pint Chicken or Vegetable Stock, chilled (see page 122)*

*300 ml/½ pint natural yogurt*

*1 teaspoon fresh lemon juice*

*½ teaspoon white pepper, or more to taste*

*salt to taste*

*To garnish:*

*4–6 slices of cucumber, cut wafter-thin*

*1 teaspoon snipped fresh dill*

*paprika*

# Consommé

This classic soup is the foundation for a number of variations. It can be served hot or chilled. If chilled it will turn to jelly, in which case it should be broken up with a fork before serving and sprinkled with finely chopped fresh green herbs such as parsley, chervil or chives. Consommé is an ideal starter if followed by a substantial second course.

**1** Cut the meat into small pieces and place it in a large saucepan. Add the beef stock, onion, celery, parsley and peppercorns. Bring the mixture to the boil, then lower the heat and simmer, partially covered, for 1½ hours. Carefully strain the liquid through a muslin cloth or very fine wire sieve into another saucepan. Add the sherry, if using.

**2** To clear the consommé add the egg white and crushed shell. Simmer for a further 30 minutes, then strain again.

**3** Return the consommé to the clean pan, and add the sugar and salt, if using. Heat, stirring until the sugar has dissolved. Serve the consommé in bouillon cups, hot or well chilled.

*375 g/12 oz lean shin of beef*

*1. litres/2 pints Beef Stock (see page 120)*

*1 onion, chopped coarsely*

*1 celery stick, sliced*

*2 sprigs of parsley*

*6 black peppercorns*

*1 tablespoon medium dry sherry (optional)*

*white of 1 egg, lightly beaten*

*shell of 1 egg, lightly crushed*

*1 lump or 1 teaspoon of sugar*

*salt (optional)*

- Serves 6
- Preparation time: 10–15 minutes
- Cooking time: about 2 hours

## Variation

# Consommé Royal

Follow the main recipe for hot consomme, but add the following garnish: Whisk 2 egg yolks lightly in a bowl, then add the 1 whole egg and the milk. Mix well and season with salt and pepper. Cover the bowl tightly with greaseproof paper and steam in a saucepan of boiling water for 15–20 minutes. Leave to cool, then cut the mixture into julienne strips or small dice. Sprinkle the strips or cubes on individual portions of the hot consommé.

**To garnish:**
**yolks of 2 eggs**
**1 whole egg**
**150 ml/¼ pint milk**
**salt and pepper**

- Serves 6
- Preparation time: 20–25 minutes
- Cooking time: about 2½ hours

## Variation

# Consommé with Egg Rain

Follow the main recipe for hot consommé, but add the following garnish. In a small bowl whisk 2 eggs with the milk. Add salt and pepper to taste.
Bring the consommé to the boil. Slowly run the egg mixture through a coarse sieve into the boiling soup. Continue to boil for 1 minute then serve in heated bowls.

**To garnish:**
**2 eggs**
**75 ml/3 fl oz milk**
**salt and pepper**

- Serves 6
- Preparation time: 20 minutes
- Cooking time: about 2 hours

# Mint, Cucumber and Green Pea Soup

This soup, illustrated opposite, is equally delicious served hot or cold.

**1** Melt the butter or margarine in a large saucepan. Cook the chopped cucumber over a moderate heat, stirring occasionally, for 5 minutes. Add the peas, sugar, pepper and 2 tablespoons of the mint. Pour in the stock. Bring the mixture to the boil, then add the potatoes. Lower the heat and simmer, partially covered, for about 20 minutes, or until the potatoes are tender.

**2** In a blender or food processor purée the mixture in batches until smooth, transferring each successive batch to another saucepan or, if the soup is to be served cold, to a bowl. Season with salt.

**3** If the soup is to be served hot, add the cream and reheat gently without boiling. Serve in heated bowls, garnishing each portion with a little of the remaining chopped mint. If the soup is to be served cold, cover the bowl closely and refrigerate for at least 3 hours. Just before serving fold in the chilled cream. Serve in chilled bowls, garnishing each portion with the mint.

*50 g/2 oz butter or margarine*

*500 g/1 lb cucumbers, peeled and deseeded, cut into 1 cm/½ inch pieces*

*250 g/8 oz shelled fresh or frozen peas*

*pinch of sugar*

*¼ teaspoon white pepper*

*3 tablespoons finely chopped fresh mint*

*1.2 litres/2 pints Chicken or Vegetable Stock (see page 122)*

*175 g/6 oz potatoes, peeled and chopped coarsely*

*salt*

*150 ml/¼ pint double cream (chilled, if the soup is to be served cold)*

- Serves 6
- Preparation time: 15 minutes, plus 3 hours chilling time (if serving cold)
- Cooking time: 25–30 minutes

# Chilled Avocado Soup

This delicately flavoured, easy-to-prepare soup must not be left for longer than 1 hour before it is served, or it will lose its subtle, pale green colour. Make sure that all the ingredients are well chilled.

**1** Chill the soup bowls in the freezer. Cut the avocados in half and remove the stones. Remove the peel and slice the avocados into a blender or food processor, discarding any discoloured flesh.

**2** Add the lemon juice and yogurt, with 600 ml/1 pint of the stock and process the mixture to a very smooth purée. Transfer the purée to a bowl.

**3** Whisk in the cream, then add the remaining stock, cayenne and white pepper with salt to taste. Stir well, cover closely and chill for 1 hour in the refrigerator.

**4** Serve the soup in well chilled bowls, sprinkling each portion with snipped chives to garnish.

- Serves 4
- Preparation time: about 5 minutes, plus 1 hour chilling time

*2 large ripe avocados*

*1 teaspoon lemon juice*

*150 ml/¼ pint natural yogurt*

*750 ml/1¼ pints Chicken Stock (see page 122), chilled*

*4 tablespoons single cream, chilled*

*cayenne pepper*

*¼ teaspoon white pepper*

*salt*

*2 tablespoons snipped fresh chives, to garnish*

## Variation

# Avocado Soup with Lemon and Tabasco

Proceed as in the main recipe but in step 2, add 2 tablespoons of fresh lemon juice, 2 teaspoons of finely grated lemon zest and a few drops of Tabasco sauce, together with the yogurt and stock. Purée according to the instructions in the main recipe. This soup can be garnished with grated lemon zest instead of the chives.

- Serves 4
- Preparation time: about 5 minutes, plus 1 hour chilling time

*2 tablespoons fresh lemon juice*

*2 teaspoons finely grated lemon zest*

*a few drops of Tabasco sauce*

*grated lemon zest, to garnish*

# Chilled Fresh Fruit Soup

## Variation

## *Chilled Fruit Soup*

Replace the pears with the same quantity of peaches, apricots or plums. If fresh strawberries are unavailable substitute frozen strawberries. Defrost well before use. Proceed as in the main recipe.

- Serves 6
- Preparation time: 10 minutes, plus
  3–4 hours chilling time

On a sweltering summer's day this healthy concoction of fruit, juices and honey is an ideal replacement for breakfast, or even lunch.

**1** Place all the fruit in a blender or food processor with 300 ml/½ pint of the orange juice and blend until very smooth. Add the lemon juice and grapefruit juice and the honey. Blend again until the mixture is reduced to a purée. It may be necessary to do this in batches.

**2** Pour the soup into a large bowl, stir in the remaining orange juice and cover the bowl closely. Chill in the refrigerator for 3–4 hours.

**3** Pour the chilled soup into 6 chilled bowls and garnish each portion with a sprig of fresh mint and a strawberry.

- Serves 6
- Preparation time: 10 minutes, plus 3–4 hours chilling time

*2 dessert apples, peeled, quartered and cored*

*6 bananas, roughly chopped*

*500 g/1 lb fresh strawberries*

*375 g/12 oz pears, peeled, quartered and cored*

*1 litre/1¾ pints fresh orange juice*

*2 tablespoons lemon juice*

*300 ml/½ pint fresh grapefruit juice*

*5–6 tablespoons clear honey*

*To garnish:*

*sprigs of fresh mint*

*6 strawberries*

# Winter Soups

There is nothing more welcome than a
bowl of hot soup on a cold winter's day.
The recipes in this chapter are all easy to
make and all use ingredients which are
readily available, particularly in
the winter months. Each recipe will
fill the home with delicious smells of
home-cooking and encourage anyone
to the table.

# Armenian Onion and Lentil Soup

This hearty winter soup is illustrated on pages 30–31.

1 Wash the barley in a colander under cold running water. Drain well, tip into a saucepan and add 150 ml/¼ pint water. Bring the mixture to the boil. Lower the heat and simmer, partially covered, for 25–30 minutes, or until all the water is absorbed. Stir occasionally.

2 Add the stock, onions, lentils, tarragon, paprika, cayenne pepper, sugar and white wine. Bring the mixture to the boil, lower the heat and simmer, partially covered, for about 1¼ hours. Add a little more water if the soup is too thick. Season with salt and pepper.

3 Melt the butter for the garnish in a small frying pan over a moderate heat. Add the finely chopped onion and cook, stirring occasionally, for 5 minutes or until the onion is soft and golden.

4 Carefully ladle the soup into heated bowls or deep soup plates, garnish with the fried onion and serve.

- Serves: 8
- Preparation time: 15 minutes
- Cooking time: about 1¾ hours

*25 g/1 oz pearl barley*

*1.8 litres/3 pints Beef Stock (see page 120)*

*500 g/1 lb onions, sliced thinly*

*150 g/5 oz green lentils, washed, drained and picked over*

*1 teaspoon dried tarragon*

*2 teaspoons paprika*

*pinch of cayenne pepper*

*¼ teaspoon sugar*

*3 tablespoons dry white wine*

*salt and pepper*

*To garnish:*

*25 g/1 oz butter or margarine*

*3 tablespoons finely chopped mild onion*

# French Onion Soup

There are several varieties of onion: larger and milder ones grow in warmer climates, while smaller and more strongly flavoured varieties thrive in cooler regions. Colours range from white, yellow, light brown to purple red. For soups the mild and slightly sweet Spanish onion is the most suitable.

1 Peel the onions, discard the skins and slice them into fairly thick even rings.

2 Melt the butter or margarine in a heavy-bottomed saucepan. Add the onions and cook over a moderate heat, stirring constantly, until soft and pale gold in colour. Sprinkle in the flour, stir for about 1 minute, then gradually pour in the stock. Bring the mixture to the boil, stirring constantly. Add salt and pepper to taste.

3 Lower the heat and simmer for 20–25 minutes. Add the cognac, if using. Stir in the Dijon mustard. Keep the onion soup hot.

4 Grill the bread for the garnish until it is lightly browned. Sprinkle each slice with grated Gruyère cheese. Pour the soup into heatproof bowls, float a slice of cheese-topped bread in each portion. Put the bowls under a preheated grill until the cheese melts and bubbles. Serve immediately.

- Serves 6
- Preparation time: 10 minutes
- Cooking time: about 35 minutes

*500 g/1 lb Spanish onions*

*50 g/2 oz butter or margarine*

*25 g/1 oz plain flour*

*1.2 litres/2 pints Beef Stock (see page 120)*

*1 tablespoon cognac (optional)*

*½ teaspoon Dijon mustard*

*salt and pepper*

*To garnish:*

*6 slices French bread*

*75 g/3 oz Gruyère cheese, grated*

32

# White Onion Soup

1 Peel the onions and slice them into fairly thick rings.
2 Melt the butter or margarine in a heavy-bottomed saucepan. Add the onions and cook over a high heat for 3 minutes, stirring constantly. Do not allow them to brown. Stir in the flour and cook for 1 minute, then gradually stir in the boiling water.
3 Add salt and white pepper to taste. Cook over a moderate heat for 10 minutes. Stirring from time to time. Gradually add the milk, stirring constantly. Cover the pan and simmer the soup over a very gentle heat for 15–20 minutes, or until the onions are very soft. Taste and adjust the seasoning, if necessary, and add the cream before serving in heated bowls.

*6 Spanish onions*
*50 g/2 oz butter or margarine*
*1 tablespoon plain flour*
*300 ml/½ pint boiling water*
*1 litre/1¾ pints warm milk*
*salt and white pepper*
*1 tablespoon single cream*

- Serves 6
- Preparation time: 10–12 minutes
- Cooking time: 30–35 minutes

# Heart of Artichoke Soup with Dill

1 Melt the butter or margarine in a saucepan. Add the onion, garlic and celery. Cook, covered, over a moderate heat for 10–12 minutes, or until all the vegetables are soft. Stir from time to time.
2 Add the artichoke hearts, replace the lid and cook for about 3 minutes more. Pour in 1 litre/1¾ pints of the stock and the lemon juice. Stir in 1 tablespoon of the dill and then cook, covered, over a moderate heat for 15 minutes.
3 In a blender or food processor purée the mixture in batches until smooth, transferring each successive batch to a clean saucepan.
4 Mix the flour with the remaining stock in a small bowl, adding a little water if necessary. Reheat the soup, whisk in the flour mixture and stir until the soup thickens slightly. Add the remaining dill, season with salt and pepper, then add the cream. Heat thoroughly but do not allow the soup to boil or it will curdle. Serve in heated soup plates or bowls. Garnish each portion with a sprig of dill.

*50 g/2 oz butter or margarine*
*1 onion, chopped*
*1 garlic clove, chopped*
*1 celery stick, sliced*
*1 x 425 g/14 oz can artichoke hearts, drained*
*1.2 litres/2 pints Chicken or Vegetable Stock (see page 122)*
*1 tablespoon fresh lemon juice*
*3 tablespoons snipped fresh dill*
*2 tablespoons plain flour*
*150 ml/¼ pint single cream*
*salt and ground white pepper*
*4–6 sprigs of dill, to garnish*

- Serves 4–6
- Preparation time: 15–20 minutes
- Cooking time: about 35 minutes

# Bacon and Turnip Soup

**1** Melt the butter or margarine in a heavy-bottomed saucepan, add the bacon and cook over a moderate heat until crisp and golden. Remove the bacon with a slotted spoon and set aside.

**2** Cook the onion, potatoes and turnips in the bacon fat for about 5 minutes over a low heat. Add the stock, bay leaf and thyme. Bring to the boil, then lower the heat and cook for 30–35 minutes, or until all the vegetables are soft. Remove and discard the bay leaf and sprig of thyme, if used.

**3** In a blender or food processor purée the mixture in batches until smooth. Transfer each successive batch to a clean saucepan. Add the reserved bacon and the milk. Cook over a moderate heat for 35 minutes, or until the soup is hot, but not boiling. Stir frequently. Serve at once in heated soup plates or bowls. Sprinkle each portion with a little finely chopped parsley.

- Serves 6
- Preparation time: 10–12 minutes
- Cooking time: 45 minutes

*25 g/1 oz butter or margarine*

*125 g/4 oz rindless smoked bacon, chopped coarsely*

*1 onion, chopped*

*375 g/12 oz potatoes, peeled and chopped*

*750 g/1½ lb turnips, peeled and chopped*

*1.2 litres/2 pints Chicken Stock (see page 122)*

*1 bay leaf*

*1 small sprig of thyme, or ¼ teaspoon dried thyme*

*150 ml/¼ pint milk*

*salt and pepper*

*finely chopped parsley, to garnish*

# Sweet Potato Soup

Smooth in texture, delicate in taste, this is a comforting winter soup for both children and adults alike. It is illustrated opposite.

**1** Heat the bacon in a frying pan over a gentle heat until the fat runs, then raise the heat and fry over a moderate heat until very crisp. Using tongs, transfer the bacon on to kitchen paper to drain.

**2** Add the butter or margarine to the bacon fat remaining in the frying pan and cook the onion, carrots, celery and bay leaf over a low heat for 5–8 minutes, stirring frequently.

**3** Transfer the mixture to a saucepan. Add the sweet potatoes, potatoes, stock, 150 ml/¼ pint water and white wine. Bring the mixture to the boil, then lower the heat and simmer, covered, for about 35–40 minutes, or until the vegetables are very tender. Remove the bay leaf.

**4** In a blender or food processor, blend the mixture in batches until smooth, transferring each successive batch to a clean saucepan. Add the nutmeg, white pepper and salt to taste. Place the pan over a moderate heat, stirring until the soup is hot.

**5** Serve the soup in heated bowls. Crumble a little of the reserved bacon over each portion to garnish.

- Serves 6–8
- Preparation time: 15 minutes
- Cooking time: 50 minutes

*4–6 rashers of rindless smoked bacon*

*25 g/1 oz butter or margarine*

*1 onion, chopped*

*2 carrots, sliced*

*2 celery sticks, sliced*

*1 bay leaf*

*750 g/1½ lb sweet potato, peeled and sliced*

*250 g/8 oz peeled and sliced potato*

*1.2 litres/2 pints Chicken Stock (see page 122)*

*125 ml/4 fl oz dry white wine*

*¼ teaspoon grated nutmeg*

*¼ teaspoon white pepper*

*salt*

# Jerusalem Artichoke Soup

Through inaccurate description and wrong pronunciation the Jerusalem artichoke received its inappropriate name, for it has nothing to do with an artichoke or Jerusalem. Originally these nobbly tubers were grown by native Americans. They were discovered by French explorers in 1605 in Massachusetts.

**1** If the artichokes are fairly smooth they can be peeled, but must be dropped at once into water acidulated with lemon juice or they will discolour. If they are knobbly scrub them in plenty of water and cut off dark tips and any small dry roots. Slice the cleaned artichokes and drop them into acidulated water immediately.

**2** Melt the butter or margarine in a saucepan. Add the onion and cook until soft. Stir in the artichokes and cook over a moderate heat for 3 minutes, stirring constantly. Add salt and pepper to taste. Pour in the stock and milk and bring the mixture to simmering point, stirring all the time. Partially cover the pan and simmer for 30 minutes, or until the vegetables are tender.

**3** In a blender or food processor, blend the mixture very briefly in batches to a coarse purée, transferring each successive batch to a clean saucepan. Reheat gently and stir in the cream. Do not allow the soup to boil. Serve hot in warmed soup bowls or plates, garnished with finely chopped parsley and croûtons.

- Serves 6–8
- Preparation time: 15 minutes
- Cooking time: about 35 minutes

*1 kg/2 lb Jerusalem artichokes*

*lemon juice*

*50 g/2 oz butter or margarine*

*1 onion, chopped*

*600 ml/1 pint Chicken or Vegetable Stock (see page 122)*

*600 ml/1 pint milk*

*150 ml/¼ pint single cream*

*salt and ground white pepper*

*To garnish:*

*finely chopped fresh parsley*

*croûtons (see page 66)*

# Parsnip and Orange Soup

The humble, inexpensive parsnip can be transformed into a number of delicious soups.

**1** Melt the butter or margarine in a large saucepan. Add the parsnips, onion and potato with grated nutmeg if using. Cook over a low to moderate heat, covered, for 10 minutes. Stir occasionally.

**2** Add the orange juice, orange strips and stock. Bring to the boil, then lower the heat, cover the pan and simmer for 30 minutes. Remove and discard the orange strips.

**3** In a blender or food processor, purée the mixture in batches, transferring each successive batch to a clean saucepan. If the mixture is too thick, add a little water.

**4** Mix the lemon juice with the cream in a jug or bowl and stir it into the soup. Heat very gently without boiling, or the soup will curdle. Season with salt and white pepper to taste. Serve at once in heated soup bowls. Garnish each portion with an orange segment.

- Serves 6-8
- Preparation time: 15 minutes
- Cooking time: about 40 minutes

*125 g/4 oz butter or margarine*

*1.5 kg/3 lb parsnips, scrubbed and chopped coarsely*

*1 onion, chopped*

*1 potato, peeled and chopped*

*grated nutmeg (optional)*

*150 ml/¼ pint freshly squeezed orange juice*

*pared rind of 1 orange, cut into wide strips*

*1.8 litres/3 pints Chicken or Vegetable Stock (see page 122)*

*1 teaspoon lemon juice*

*125 ml/4 fl oz double cream*

*salt and white pepper*

*6-8 orange segments, to garnish*

## *Variation*

## *Curried Parsnip Soup*

1 Melt the butter or margarine in a large saucepan. Add the parsnips, onion, potato, curry powder, turmeric and cumin and stir well. Cover the pan and cook the mixture over a low to moderate heat for 10 minutes. Stir occasionally.

2 Pour in the chicken or vegetable stock and bring the mixture to the boil. Lower the heat, replace the lid and cook for 30 minutes over a moderate heat. Add a little water if the mixture is too thick.

3 In a blender or food processor purée the mixture in batches, transferring each successive batch to a clean saucepan. Heat the soup gently and stir in the cream. Serve at once in heated soup bowls or plates. Garnish each portion with a sprinkling of chives or parsley.

*125 g/4 oz butter or margarine*

*1.5 kg/3 lb parsnips, scrubbed and chopped coarsely*

*1 onion, chopped*

*1 potato, peeled and chopped*

*1 tablespoon medium hot curry powder*

*1 teaspoon ground turmeric*

*½ teaspoon ground cumin*

*1.8 litres/3 pints Chicken or Vegetable Stock (see pages 122)*

*150 ml/¼ pint double cream*

*salt and pepper*

*snipped fresh chives or finely chopped fresh parsley, to garnish*

- Serves 6–8
- Preparation time: 15 minutes
- Cooking time: about 40 minutes

# Parsnip and Fennel Soup

1 Melt the butter or margarine in a large saucepan. Add the parsnips, fennel and onion. Cook over a moderate heat for 15 minutes, or until the vegetables are soft, stirring constantly.

2 In a small bowl mix the cornflour with 150 ml/¼ pint of the hot chicken or vegetable stock until thick and smooth. Fold the mixture into the vegetables, then pour in the hot stock. Stir the soup constantly.

3 Bring the mixture to the boil, lower the heat and simmer, partially covered, for 20 minutes. Stir frequently. Add salt and pepper to taste, stir in the cream and heat through without boiling. Serve at once in heated soup bowls or plates.

*50 g/2 oz butter or margarine*

*500 g/1 lb parsnips, scrubbed and cut into 5 mm/¼ inch dice*

*500 g/1 lb fennel bulb, cut into small pieces of equal size*

*1 onion, chopped*

*3 tablespoons cornflour*

*1.2 litres/2 pints hot Chicken or Vegetable Stock (see page 122)*

*150 ml/¼ pint double cream*

*salt and pepper*

- Serves 4–6
- Preparation time: 10–15 minutes
- Cooking time: 25–30 minutes

37

# Bortsch

This tangy beetroot soup, illustrated opposite, is part of the staple diet of both Russia and Poland. Like most national dishes Bortsch has a great number of variations. This is a simplified version, which makes a delicious winter starter.

**1** Place the beetroot in a saucepan, cover with plenty of cold water and add 1 tablespoon of salt. Bring to the boil, lower the heat, cover and simmer steadily for 35–45 minutes. Drain, discarding the liquid, then rinse the beetroot under cold water, dry with kitchen paper and slip off the skins.

**2** Grate the beetroot into a large saucepan. Add the tomatoes, the beef stock, cabbage leaves, 2 teaspoons of salt, bay leaf, caraway seeds, peppercorns, vinegar and sugar. Stir well. Bring the mixture to the boil, lower the heat, cover the pan and simmer gently for about 1½ hours, or until the beef is tender.

**3** Remove and discard the bay leaf. Remove the beef and reserve it for use in another recipe. Drop the potatoes into the soup and continue simmering until the potatoes are tender, but not too soft. Serve the soup hot in heated soup plates. Garnish each portion of soup with a teaspoon of soured cream.

*4 raw beetroot*

*4 tomatoes, skinned and chopped*

*1.2 litres/2 pints Beef Stock (see page 120)*

*3 large cabbage leaves, shredded coarsely*

*1 bay leaf*

*½ teaspoon caraway seeds*

*6 black peppercorns, crushed*

*5 tablespoons red wine vinegar*

*2 tablespoons sugar*

*6 small potatoes, peeled*

*salt*

*6 teaspoons soured cream, to garnish*

- Serves 6
- Preparation time: 15 minutes
- Cooking time: about 2¼ hours, including cooking the beetroot

# Brussels Sprouts Soup

A comforting winter soup. The use of bacon and celery counteracts the strong flavour of the Brussels sprouts.

**1** Melt the oil in a heavy-bottomed saucepan. Add the bacon and cook over a moderate heat until golden. Add the onion and celery and cook, covered, over a moderate heat for 5 minutes, stirring frequently. Add the Brussels sprouts and cook for 5–8 minutes more.

**2** Add 900 ml/1½ pints water, potatoes, marjoram and the nutmeg. Cook, uncovered, for about 30 minutes over a moderate heat. Add salt and pepper to taste.

**3** In a blender or food processor, purée the mixture in batches until it is smooth. Transfer each successive batch to a clean saucepan.

**4** In a small bowl blend the egg yolk with the milk. Bring the soup to simmering point and reheat thoroughly, then stir in the egg and milk mixture. Do not allow the soup to boil or it will curdle.

- Serves 4–6
- Preparation time: 15 minutes
- Cooking time: 35–40 minutes

*1 tablespoon olive oil*

*50 g/2 oz rindless unsmoked streaky bacon, finely chopped*

*1 onion, chopped*

*1 celery stick, sliced thinly*

*375 g/12 oz Brussels sprouts, trimmed and chopped*

*375 g/12 oz potatoes, peeled and cut into 1 cm/½ inch cubes*

*1 teaspoon finely chopped marjoram, or ½ teaspoon dried marjoram*

*pinch of grated nutmeg, or to taste*

*1 egg yolk*

*4 tablespoons milk*

*salt and white pepper*

# Cheddar Cheese Soup

**1** Melt the butter or margarine in a heavy-bottomed saucepan. Add the onion and cook over a moderate heat for 5 minutes until transparent but not golden. Stir frequently. Add the flour and stir until the mixture is well blended. Gradually add the warm chicken stock, stirring all the time until the mixture boils and thickens.

**2** Lower the heat and stir in the milk, cheese and pepper with salt to taste. Cook over a low heat, stirring constantly until the cheese is melted and the soup begins to bubble. Serve immediately in heated bowls.

- Serves 6
- Preparation time: 10 minutes
- Cooking time: 10–15 minutes

*50 g/2 oz butter or margarine*

*1 onion, grated finely*

*25 g/1 oz plain flour*

*1 litre/1¾ pints warm Chicken Stock (see page 122)*

*450 ml/¾ pint milk*

*250 g/8 oz Cheddar cheese, grated*

*½ teaspoon white pepper*

*salt*

**40**

# Cream of Celeriac Soup

Choose the smoothest looking root to avoid a lot of waste, and cut it into pieces so that it is easier to peel. This is a light soup, but full of unusual flavour.

**I** Place the stock in a large saucepan with the bay leaf, nutmeg and pepper. Bring the liquid to the boil.

**2** Add the celeriac and potatoes, with salt to taste. Bring to the boil again, then lower the heat and simmer, partially covered, for about 35 minutes or until the all vegetables are soft. Then remove and discard the bay leaf.

**3** In a blender or food processor blend the mixture in batches, transferring each successive batch to a clean saucepan. Reheat the soup gently and stir in the cream. Do not allow the soup to boil. Serve in heated soup bowls or plates. Sprinkle each portion with finely chopped parsley to garnish.

*1.2 litres/2 pints Chicken or Vegetable Stock (see page 122)*

*I bay leaf*

*pinch of grated nutmeg*

*¼ teaspoon ground white pepper*

*I celeriac, about 750 g/ 1½ lb, peeled and cubed*

*375 g/12 oz potatoes, peeled and cubed*

*250 ml/8 fl oz single cream*

*salt*

*finely chopped fresh parsley, to garnish*

- Serves 4–6
- Preparation time: 10–15 minutes
- Cooking time: about 45 minutes

Variation

## Celeriac and Apple Soup

**I** Melt the butter or margarine in a large saucepan and sweat the celeriac and apples over a moderate heat for 5 minutes or until the vegetables have begun to soften.

**2** Add the stock and cayenne pepper and bring to the boil. Lower the heat and simmer, covered, for 25–30 minutes, or until the celeriac and apples are very soft.

**3** In a blender or food processor, purée the mixture in batches until it is very smooth, transferring each successive batch to a clean saucepan. Reheat gently. Season to taste with salt and pepper. Serve hot in heated soup bowls or plates. Garnish each portion with the finely diced apple and a dusting of paprika.

*50 g/2 oz butter or margarine*

*I celeriac, about 500 g/1 lb, peeled and cubed*

*3 dessert apples, peeled, cored and chopped*

*1.2 litres/2 pints Chicken or Vegetable Stock (see page 122)*

*pinch of cayenne pepper, or more to taste*

*salt and ground white pepper*

*To garnish:*

*2-3 tablespoons finely diced dessert apple*

*paprika*

- Serves 4–6
- Preparation time: 10–15 minutes
- Cooking time: about 35 minutes

# Jamaican Pepperpot Soup

Although imported from the sunny Caribbean this wholesome soup, illustrated opposite, is a perfect dish for a gloomy winter's day.

**1** Combine the meat with 2.4 litres/4 pints water in a large saucepan. Bring to the boil, then lower the heat and simmer the meat, partially covered, for about 30 minutes.

**2** Meanwhile prepare all the vegetables. Cut away and discard the conical part from the stalk ends of the okra and chop the okra coarsely. Set aside. Remove and discard the stems from the kale, chop the leaves coarsely and set aside. Remove and discard the stems from the spinach, chop all the leaves coarsely and set aside. Core, deseed, chop the peppers coarsely and reserve. Roughly chop the spring onions. Peel the yams and the potato, slice both thinly and set aside with the other vegetables. Crush or finely chop the garlic.

**3** Add the okra, kale, spinach, peppers and spring onions to the soup with the thyme and cayenne. Cook over a moderate heat, partially covered, for 15 minutes. Add the yams, potato and garlic and cook for a further 20 minutes, or until the yams and potato are soft. Add more water if the soup is too thick. Season with salt. Serve hot in a heated soup tureen.

*1 kg/2 lb lean stewing beef, cut into small cubes*

*250 g/8 oz lean pork, cut into small cubes*

*24 okra*

*500 g/1 lb kale*

*500 g/1 lb spinach*

*2 green peppers*

*2 spring onions*

*500 g/1 lb yellow yams*

*1 large potato*

*1 garlic clove*

*1 sprig of fresh thyme, or ¼ teaspoon dried thyme*

*¼ teaspoon cayenne pepper*

*salt*

- Serves 6–8
- Preparation time: 30–35 minutes
- Cooking time: about 1¼ hours

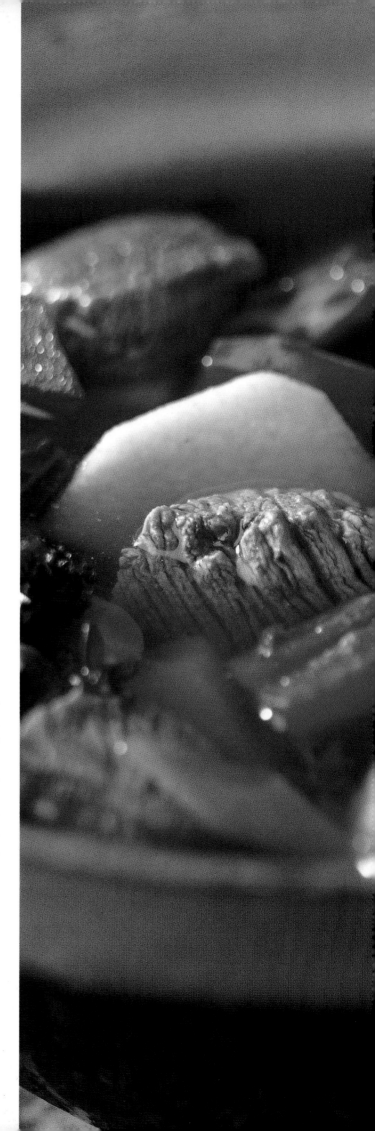

# Beef and Cabbage Soup with Dijon Mustard

**1** Heat the oil in a heavy-bottomed saucepan. Add the meat and cook, over a moderate to high heat for 2 minutes, turning each piece over once. Add the onions and cook over a moderate heat for 3 minutes. Stir frequently.

**2** Add the stock, caraway seeds, marjoram and thyme. Bring the mixture to the boil, then lower the heat and simmer, partially covered, for 35–40 minutes. Add the potatoes and cabbage and cook, partially covered, for 25 minutes more.

**3** Using a slotted spoon, transfer the meat to a board. When cool enough to handle, cut it into 1 cm/½ inch dice. Return the meat to the soup. Stir in the mustard and cook for 2 minutes without allowing the soup to boil. Serve the soup in heated bowls.

- Serves 4–6
- Preparation time: about 15 minutes
- Cooking time: 1¼ hours

*2 tablespoons olive oil*

*250 g/8 oz lean beef, in 1 or 2 pieces*

*2 onions, chopped finely*

*1.5 litres/2½ pints Beef Stock (see page 120)*

*2 teaspoons caraway seeds*

*1 teaspoon chopped fresh marjoram, or ½ teaspoon dried marjoram*

*½ teaspoon chopped fresh thyme, or ¼ teaspoon dried thyme*

*175 g/6 oz potatoes, peeled and diced*

*175–200 g/6–7 oz Savoy cabbage, finely shredded*

*1 tablespoon Dijon mustard*

## Variation

# Beef and Cabbage Soup with Tomato and Caraway

Follow the main recipe up to step 3, but omit the 1 tablespoon of Dijon mustard. Instead stir in 2 tablespoons of tomato purée when adding the potatoes and Savoy cabbage to the soup.

- Serves 4–6
- Preparation time: about 15 minutes
- Cooking time: 1¼ hours

**44**

# Hungarian Sauerkraut Soup

The unique blend of sweet paprika, tangy sauerkraut and fragrant caraway seeds give this soup a very distinctive taste. Use sweet Hungarian paprika if you can find it.

**1** Melt the butter or margarine in a heavy-bottomed saucepan and cook the onion over a moderate heat until it is softened but not brown.

**2** Add the sauerkraut, paprika and caraway seeds and cook for a further 2 minutes, stirring constantly. Add the stock, tomato purée, caster sugar and potatoes. Stir and bring the mixture to the boil. Season to taste with salt. Lower the heat and simmer, covered, for about 45 minutes.

**3** In a small bowl mix the soured cream with the chives. Serve the soup immediately in heated bowls garnishing each portion with 1 tablespoon of the soured cream mixture.

- Serves 6
- Preparation time: 10 minutes
- Cooking time: 50 minutes

*50 g/2 oz butter or margarine*

*1 large onion, chopped*

*1 x 475–500 g/15–16 oz can or jar sauerkraut, drained and chopped*

*2 tablespoons paprika*

*1 tablespoon caraway seeds*

*1.5 litres/2½ pints Vegetable or Chicken Stock (see page 122)*

*2 tablespoons tomato purée*

*¼ teaspoon caster sugar*

*375 g/12 oz potatoes, peeled and diced*

*salt*

*To garnish:*

*4–6 tablespoons soured cream*

*1–2 tablespoons snipped fresh chives*

# Game Broth

**1** Melt the butter or margarine in a large saucepan. Add the game trimmings or leftovers with the beef, ham, onion, celery and carrot. Set the breast of game aside. Place the pan over moderate heat and cook for 5 minutes, or until the vegetables begin to brown. Stir frequently.

**2** Add the stock, bouquet garni, bay leaf, juniper berries, peppercorns and parsley to the pan. Bring the mixture to the boil, lower the heat and simmer, partially covered, for about 2 hours. Add more water if the liquid reduces too much.

**3** Strain the liquid through a fine sieve into a clean pan. Discard the solids in the sieve. Stir the sherry into the broth and season with salt, then add the reserved strips of cooked breast of game. Simmer until heated through. Serve the broth in heated soup bowls.

- Serves 6–8
- Preparation time: about 15 minutes
- Cooking time: about 2 hours

*50 g/2 oz butter or margarine*

*500 g/1 lb cooked game, trimmings or leftovers, plus 250 g/8 oz cooked breast of game, cut into thin strips*

*250 g/8 oz raw lean beef, thinly cut across the grain*

*50 g/2 oz lean cooked ham, chopped finely*

*1 onion, chopped*

*1 celery stick, sliced*

*1 carrot, chopped*

*2 litres/3½ pints Beef Stock (see page 120)*

*1 bouquet garni*

*1 bay leaf*

*3 juniper berries*

*6 black peppercorns*

*2 sprigs of parsley*

*2 tablespoons dry sherry*

*salt*

# Vegetable Soups

The soups in this chapter range from
hearty winter vegetable soups to
delicate, light chilled soups. Most of the
soups here are suitable for
vegetarians or can be adapted to be so.
Just ensure that vegetable stock is used
and use a vegetarian cheese when
cheese is called for.

# Pumpkin Soup

The bright orange pumpkin is popular in Caribbean and American cooking and is used as both a fruit and a vegetable. Pumpkins have a delicate flavour and are low in calories. This delicious recipe is illustrated on pages 46–47.

**1** Melt the butter or margarine in a large saucepan. Add the pumpkin. Stir well and cook over a low to moderate heat for 10 minutes. Add 150 ml/¼ pint warm water, the nutmeg and the thyme with salt and pepper to taste. Cover and cook quickly over a high heat until the pumpkin is soft.

**2** In a blender or food processor purée the pumpkin mixture, with a little milk if necessary, until smooth. It may be necessary to do this in batches. Scrape the purée into a clean saucepan.

**3** Add the remaining milk and rice to the pumpkin purée in the pan. Stir well and cook, covered, for 30 minutes or until the rice is tender. Stir from time to time. Serve the pumpkin soup in heated bowls garnished with croûtons.

*50 g/2 oz butter or margarine*

*750 g/1½ lb pumpkin, peeled, deseeded and cut into large pieces*

*¼ teaspoon grated nutmeg*

*pinch of dried thyme*

*1.5 litres/2½ pints milk*

*50 g/2 oz long-grain rice*

*salt and white pepper*

*croûtons (see page 66), to garnish*

- Serves 6
- Preparation time: about 10 minutes
- Cooking time: 40–45 minutes

*croûtons (see page 66), to garnish*

## Variation

# Gingered Pumpkin Soup

Follow the main recipe but fry the pumpkin with the finely chopped fresh root ginger. Omit the grated nutmeg and the dried thyme. Continue as in the main recipe. Garnish the soup with 4 tablespoons of pumpkin seeds, toasted under a hot grill for about 5 minutes until evenly browned.

*50 g/2 oz butter or margarine*

*750 g/1½ lb pumpkin, peeled, deseeded and chopped finely*

*2.5 cm/1 inch piece fresh root ginger, peeled and finely chopped*

*1.5 litres/2½ pints milk*

*salt and pepper*

*4 tablespoons pumpkin seeds, toasted, to garnish*

- Serves 6
- Preparation time: about 10 minutes
- Cooking time: 40–45 minutes

## *Variation*

# Chunky Pumpkin Soup with Bacon

**1** Melt the butter or margarine in a large saucepan. Add the pumpkin and bacon. Stir well and fry over a low to moderate heat until the bacon is cooked. Add 150 ml/¼ pint warm water, the nutmeg and the thyme with salt and pepper to taste. Bring to the boil, then cover and simmer for about 15 minutes until the pumpkin is soft.

**2** Add the milk and rice to the pan. Stir well and cook, covered, for 30 minutes or until the rice is tender. Stir from time to time. Serve the soup in heated bowls.

*50 g/2 oz butter or margarine*

*750 g/1½ lb pumpkin, peeled, deseeded and chopped finely*

*125 g/4 oz streaky bacon, derinded and chopped*

*¼ teaspoon grated nutmeg*

*pinch of dried thyme*

*1.5 litres/2½ pints milk*

*50 g/2 oz long-grain rice*

*salt and pepper*

- Serves 6
- Preparation time: about 10 minutes
- Cooking time: 40–45 minutes

# Spring Onion Soup

**1** Melt the butter or margarine in a large saucepan. Set aside the spring onions for the garnish. Add the spring onions to the pan and cook, stirring constantly for 5 minutes or until starting to soften.

**2** Sprinkle in the flour. Cook, stirring, for 1 minute, then slowly pour in the stock, whisking vigorously. Add the basil and nutmeg and season with salt and pepper. Simmer, stirring frequently, for 10 minutes, or until the soup has thickened slightly.

**3** Stir in the the cream and heat through without boiling. Serve the soup in heated bowls, garnishing each portion with a generous sprinkling of green spring onion tops.

*25 g/1 oz butter or margarine*

*250 g/8 oz spring onions, chopped finely*

*3 tablespoons plain flour*

*1.2 litres/2 pints Vegetable Stock (see page 122)*

*1 tablespoon chopped fresh basil, or 1 teaspoon dried basil*

*pinch of grated nutmeg*

*150 ml/¼ pint single cream*

*salt and black pepper*

*1 tablespoon very finely chopped green spring onion tops, to garnish*

- Serves 4–6
- Preparation time: 10 minutes
- Cooking time: about 15 minutes

# Celery Carrot and Apple Soup

The delicately fragrant flavour makes this soup, which is illustrated opposite, one of my favourites.

**1** Melt the butter or margarine in a large saucepan; add the celery, carrots and apple. Cover with a tight-fitting lid and cook over a low heat for 15 minutes, stirring occasionally.

**2** Add the stock, paprika, cayenne, basil, bay leaf and ginger. Bring to the boil, then lower the heat and simmer, partially covered, for 40–45 minutes, or until the vegetables and apple are very soft.

**3** In a blender or food processor, purée the mixture in batches for a few seconds each. Transfer each successive batch of purée to a bowl, then strain it through a sieve back into the clean pan. Season with salt and pepper to taste. Reheat the soup. Serve the soup in heated bowls and then garnishing each portion with a few chopped celery leaves and a light sprinkling of paprika.

*50 g/2 oz unsalted butter or margarine*

*500 g/1 lb celery, sliced*

*500 g/1 lb carrots, chopped*

*250 g/8 oz peeled, cored and coarsely chopped dessert apples*

*1.2 litres/2 pints Vegetable Stock (see page 122)*

*1 teaspoon paprika*

*cayenne pepper, to taste*

*1 tablespoon chopped fresh basil leaves, or 1 teaspoon dried basil*

*1 bay leaf*

*1 teaspoon freshly grated root ginger*

*salt and ground white pepper*

*To garnish:*

*chopped celery leaves*

*paprika*

- Serves 6
- Preparation time: 15 minutes
- Cooking time: 1 hour

# Chilled Celery Soup with Cumin

An unusual combination! The cumin gives a touch of richness to the light flavour of the celery.

**1** Thinly slice enough celery to yield 2 tablespoons. Set aside in a small bowl. Grate the rest of the celery in a food processor or by hand.

**2** Combine the grated celery, stock, onion, potatoes and cumin in a saucepan. Add salt to taste. Bring the mixture to the boil. Lower the heat and cook, partially covered, for 20–25 minutes.

**3** In a blender or food processor purée the mixture in batches until smooth, transferring each successive batch to a bowl. Stir in the reserved sliced celery. Cool, then cover closely and chill in the refrigerator for at least 3 hours. Just before serving stir in the soured cream. Serve in chilled bowls, garnish with finely chopped celery leaves.

*250 g/8 oz celery*

*1.2 litres/2 pints Vegetable Stock (see page 122)*

*1 onion, chopped*

*250 g/8 oz potatoes, peeled and chopped*

*1 teaspoon ground cumin*

*3 tablespoons chilled soured cream*

*salt*

*finely chopped celery leaves, to garnish*

- Serves 4–6
- Preparation time: 15 minutes, plus 3 hours chilling time
- Cooking time: 25 minutes

# Cream of Celery and Leek Soup

**1** Melt the butter or margarine in a saucepan, add the celery and leeks, cover with a tight-fitting lid and cook over a low heat for 15 minutes. Stir the mixture occasionally.

**2** Add the stock, parsley and bay leaf. Bring to the boil, then lower the heat and simmer, partially covered, for 40–45 minutes. Discard the parsley and bay leaf.

**3** In a blender or food processor purée the mixture in batches until smooth, transferring each successive batch to a bowl, then rub the mixture through a sieve into the clean pan. Add salt and pepper to taste. Reheat the soup and stir in the cream. Do not allow the soup to boil. Serve in heated soup bowls or plates, garnishing each portion with chopped celery leaves.

*50 g/2 oz butter or margarine*

*500 g/1 lb celery, sliced*

*250 g/8 oz leeks, white parts only, trimmed, cleaned and sliced*

*1.2 litres/2 pints Vegetable Stock (see page 122)*

*1 sprig of parsley*

*1 bay leaf*

*150 ml/¼ pint double cream*

*salt and white pepper*

*finely chopped celery leaves, to garnish*

- Serves 6
- Preparation time: 10–15 minutes
- Cooking time: about 1 hour

# Greens Soup

**I** Combine the kale, greens, leeks, caraway seeds, garlic and olive oil in a large saucepan. Pour in 1.8 litres/3 pints water, partially cover the saucepan, and bring the mixture to the boil. Lower the heat and simmer for 45 minutes.

**2** Drain the greens through a colander or sieve. Reserve the liquid and place the greens in a blender or food processor. Blend the greens until fairly smooth but not puréed.

**3** In a large saucepan combine 600 ml/1 pint of the reserved liquid with the wine. Cook over a low heat for 3 minutes, then whisk in the ricotta cheese, crème fraîche and yogurt. Stir well and continue to simmer for a further 3 minutes before adding the finely chopped greens. Stir in most of the remaining liquid to make a fairly thick soup.

**4** Simmer the soup, partially covered, for 20 minutes. Do not bring it to the boil or it will curdle. Stir occasionally. Season to taste with salt and white pepper. Serve the soup in heated soup bowls or plates.

- Serves 6–8
- Preparation time: 15–20 minutes
- Cooking time: about 1¼ hours

*500 g/1 lb kale, stems discarded*

*500 g/1 lb greens, chopped coarsely, stems discarded*

*250 g/8 oz leeks, trimmed, cleaned and sliced*

*1 teaspoon caraway seeds*

*3 garlic cloves, crushed*

*1 tablespoon olive oil*

*150 ml/¼ pint dry white wine*

*125 g/4 oz ricotta cheese*

*125 ml/4 fl oz crème fraîche*

*125 ml/4 fl oz natural yogurt*

*salt and white pepper*

# Parsley Soup

This, the most popular of kitchen herbs, is rich in carotene, vitamin C, iron and mineral salts. It is an inexpensive ingredient that can be transformed into a delicious soup with a very subtle flavour.

**I** Combine the parsley and 600 ml/1 pint water in a saucepan. Bring to the boil, then lower the heat, cover the pan and simmer, for 30 minutes.

**2** Rub the mixture through a sieve set over a large bowl. Discard the parsley remaining in the sieve.

**3** Melt the butter or margarine in the saucepan and cook the onion for 2–3 minutes or until soft. Add the parsley liquid and potatoes. Bring to the boil, then lower the heat and simmer, covered, for 15–20 minutes, or until the potatoes are tender.

**4** Add the nutmeg, with salt and pepper to taste. Serve the soup in heated bowls. Garnish each portion with parsley leaves.

- Serves 4
- Preparation time: 10 minutes
- Cooking time: about 55 minutes

*150 g/5 oz parsley, washed and dried on kitchen paper*

*25 g/1 oz butter or margarine*

*1 onion, chopped finely*

*425 g/14 oz potatoes, peeled and cut into 1 cm/½ inch strips*

*¼ teaspoon ground nutmeg*

*salt and white pepper*

*parsley leaves, to garnish*

# Smooth Red Bean Soup

This sweet-tasting bean with its floury texture is ideal for this delicious puréed soup, illustrated opposite.

**1** Drain the red kidney beans in a colander, rinse under cold running water and drain again.

**2** Heat the oil in a large heavy-bottomed saucepan and sweat the onion, garlic, pepper and carrot for 3–5 minutes, stirring constantly. Add the cayenne, chilli powder, thyme, bay leaf and rosemary. Stir and pour in the stock and 1.2 litres/2 pints water. Add the beans, tomato purée, and tomatoes. Stir well to break up the tomatoes. Bring the mixture to the boil, then lower the heat and simmer, partially covered, for 1¼ hours. Stir occasionally, skimming any froth that rises to the surface. Remove the bay leaf.

**3** Purée the mixture in a blender or food processor, then strain through a sieve into a clean pan. Add salt to taste. If the soup is too thick add a little water. Stir and heat thoroughly without allowing the soup to boil. Serve in warm soup bowls. Garnish each portion with a swirl of soured cream and a sprinkling of spring onion tops.

*250 g/8 oz dried red kidney beans, soaked overnight in cold water to cover*

*3 tablespoons olive oil*

*1 onion, chopped*

*2 garlic cloves, chopped*

*1 red pepper, cored, deseeded and chopped*

*1 carrot, chopped*

*¼ teaspoon cayenne pepper*

*1 teaspoon mild chilli powder*

*¼ teaspoon dried thyme*

*1 bay leaf*

*1 small sprig of fresh rosemary, or ¼ teaspoon dried rosemary*

*600 ml/1 pint Vegetable Stock (see page 122)*

*2 tablespoons tomato purée*

*1 x 397 g/14 oz can peeled plum tomatoes*

*salt*

*To garnish:*

*150 ml/¼ pint soured cream (optional)*

*2 tablespoons finely chopped spring onion tops*

- Serves 6–8
- Preparation time: 15 minutes, plus overnight soaking
- Cooking time: about 1½ hours

# Curried Cream of Broccoli Soup

There are several varieties of broccoli available. Green broccoli, or calabrese, is used in this soup.

**1** Strip off all the tough stems and leaves from the broccoli. Cut off the stalks, peel them and cut them all into 2.5 cm/1 inch pieces. Break the florets into very small pieces, and set them aside.

**2** Melt the butter or margarine in a large saucepan. Cook the onion and broccoli stalks, covered, for 5 minutes over a moderate heat. Stir frequently.

**3** Add the reserved florets, potato, curry powder and stock. Bring the mixture to the boil. Cook, partially covered, for 5 minutes. Using a slotted spoon, remove 6 or more florets for the garnish and set aside. Season with salt and pepper. Continue to cook the mixture over a moderate heat for 20 minutes, or until all the vegetables are soft.

**4** In a blender or food processor purée the mixture in batches until smooth, transferring each successive batch to a clean saucepan. Add the cream and heat thoroughly without allowing the soup to boil. Serve in heated soup bowls, garnishing each portion with the reserved florets.

*1 kg/2 lb broccoli*

*50 g/2 oz butter or margarine*

*1 onion, chopped*

*1 large potato, peeled and quartered*

*1 tablespoon medium hot curry powder*

*1.5 litres/2½ pints Vegetable Stock (see page 122)*

*150 ml/¼ pint single cream*

*salt and pepper*

- Serves 6
- Preparation time: 10–15 minutes
- Cooking time: 25 minutes

## Variation

## *Broccoli and Cheese Soup*

Follow steps 1–3 of the main recipe but omit the curry powder. Purée the mixture, return it to the saucepan and add the single cream, lemon juice, Worcestershire sauce and a few drops of Tabasco sauce. Simmer for 3–5 minutes. Do not boil, or the soup will curdle. Just before serving, stir in the grated cheese.

*125 ml/4 fl oz single cream*

*1 tablespoon lemon juice*

*1 teaspoon Worcestershire sauce*

*a few drops of Tabasco sauce, or to taste*

*125 g/4 oz mature Cheddar cheese, grated*

- Serves 6
- Preparation time: 10–15 minutes
- Cooking time: 25 minutes

**56**

# Spicy Apple and Potato Soup

The cayenne pepper adds spice and contrast to this velvety smooth soup.

**1** Melt the butter or margarine in a saucepan and cook the onion for 4–5 minutes, or until softened. Stir frequently. Add the apples and cayenne and cook for a further 2 minutes, stirring. Pour in the stock, then add the potatoes. Bring the mixture to the boil, lower the heat and simmer for 15–18 minutes, or until the apples and potatoes are very soft.

**2** In a blender or food processor purée the mixture in batches until it is very smooth, transferring each successive batch to a clean pan. Reheat the purée and stir in the hot milk. Taste and adjust the seasoning if necessary. While the soup is reheating melt the butter for the garnish in a small frying pan add the apple to the pan and sauté until crisp. Serve in heated soup bowls or plates, garnishing each portion with the apple and a light sprinkling of cayenne pepper.

*50 g/2 oz butter or margarine*

*1 small onion, chopped*

*2 dessert apples, peeled, cored and sliced*

*pinch of cayenne pepper, or more to taste*

*600 ml/1 pint Vegetable Stock (see page 122)*

*300 g/10 oz potatoes, peeled and sliced*

*300 ml/½ pint hot milk*

*salt*

*To garnish:*

*15 g/½ oz butter*

*2–3 thinly sliced apple quarters*

*cayenne pepper*

- Serves 4–6
- Preparation time: 10–15 minutes
- Cooking time: about 25 minutes

## Variation

## *Curried Apple and Potato Soup*

Follow the main recipe but replace the cayenne pepper with 1 tablespoon of medium hot curry powder.

- Serves 4–6
- Preparation time: 10–15 minutes
- Cooking time: about 25 minutes

# Curried Green Bean Soup

Garnish this soup with a swirl of cream as illustrated opposite.

**1** Melt the butter or margarine in a large saucepan and cook the garlic and onion over a moderate heat, until soft but not brown. Stir in the curry powder and then cook for a further 2 minutes.

**2** Pour in the stock. Add the marjoram, bay leaf, beans and potatoes, with salt to taste. Bring the mixture to the boil, then lower the heat, cover the pan and simmer for 45 minutes or until the vegetables are soft. Remove the bay leaf.

**3** Purée all of the mixture in a blender or food processor. Return the puréed soup to the saucepan. Stir well and heat gently, without boiling. Serve the soup in heated bowls. Garnish each portion of soup with a swirl of soured cream.

*50 g/2 oz butter or margarine*

*1 garlic clove, crushed*

*1 onion, chopped*

*1 tablespoon mild curry powder*

*1.5 litres/2½ pints Vegetable Stock (see page 122)*

*1 teaspoon chopped fresh marjoram, or ½ teaspoon dried marjoram*

*1 bay leaf*

*500 g/1 lb round green or French beans, trimmed and cut into 1 cm/½ inch pieces*

*250-300 g/8-10 oz potatoes, peeled and cubed*

*salt*

*150 ml/¼ pint soured cream, to garnish*

- Serves 6
- Preparation time: 15 minutes
- Cooking time: about 50 minutes

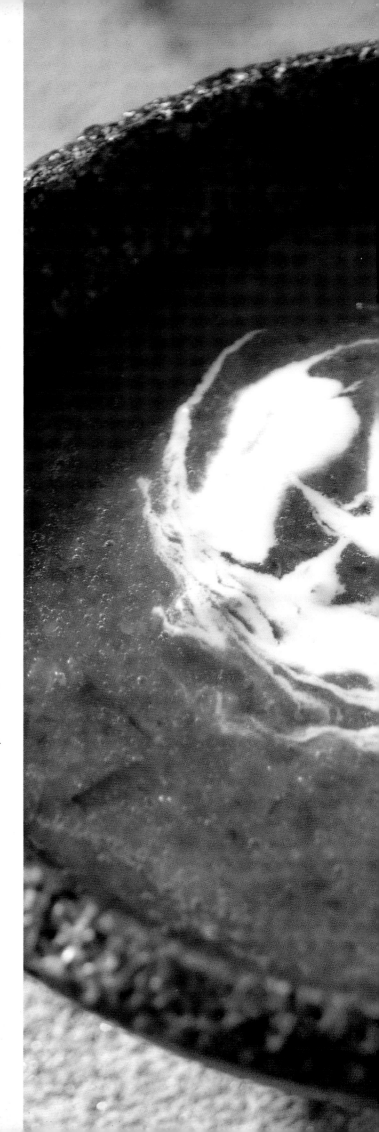

# White Bean Soup Provençal

1 Drain the beans in a colander, rinse under cold running water and drain again.

2 Heat the oil in a large saucepan and cook the garlic, pepper and onion over a moderate heat for 4–5 minutes, stirring constantly.

3 Add the tomatoes and thyme and cook for 1 minute more. Add the beans and pour in the 600 ml/1 pint water and the stock. Bring to the boil, then lower the heat, cover the pan and simmer for 1 hour.

4 Add the chopped parsley and season with salt and pepper. Serve in heated bowls.

*125 g/4 oz haricot beans, soaked overnight in water to cover*

*3 tablespoons olive oil*

*2 garlic cloves, crushed*

*1 small red pepper, cored, deseeded and chopped*

*1 onion, chopped finely*

*250 g/8 oz fresh tomatoes, chopped finely*

*1 teaspoon finely chopped fresh thyme, or ½ teaspoon dried thyme*

*600 ml/1 pint water*

*600 ml/1 pint Vegetable Stock (see page 122)*

*2 tablespoons finely chopped fresh parsley*

*salt and pepper*

- Serves 6
- Preparation time: 15–20 minutes, plus overnight soaking
- Cooking time: about 1¼ hours

# Carrot Soup

The humble, versatile carrot with its bright colour and sweetish flavour can be used in a variety of delicious soups.

1 Melt the butter or margarine in a large saucepan and cook the onion over a moderate heat until soft but not golden. Add the carrots and turnips and cook for 1 minute, stirring constantly. Pour in 900 ml/1½ pints water and the stock. Stir, then add the potatoes and sugar with salt and pepper to taste. Bring to the boil, then lower the heat, cover the pan and simmer for 25–30 minutes. Cool slightly.

*50 g/2 oz butter or margarine*

*1 onion, chopped*

*500 g/1 lb sliced carrots*

*2 turnips, diced*

*600 ml/1 pint Vegetable Stock (see page 122)*

*250 g/8 oz potatoes, peeled and sliced*

*pinch of sugar*

*salt and pepper*

*3 tablespoons double cream (optional)*

2 In a blender or food processor purée the mixture in batches until smooth. Transfer each successive batch of puréed soup to a clean saucepan.

3 Stir well and heat thoroughly without boiling. Add more pepper and salt if necessary. Just before serving stir in the cream, if liked.

- Serves 6–8
- Preparation time: 15 minutes
- Cooking time: 30–35 minutes

# Creamy Curried Carrot Soup

Follow the main recipe but add the curry powder, cumin and turmeric when cooking the carrot and turnip mixture. Stir in the cream after the soup has been puréed. Heat the soup thoroughly but do not allow it to boil or it will curdle.

- Serves 6–8
- Preparation time: 15 minutes
- Cooking time: 30–35 minutes

**50 g/2 oz butter or margarine**

**1 onion, chopped**

**500 g/1 lb sliced carrots**

**2 turnips, diced**

**600 ml/pint Vegetable Stock (see page 122)**

**250 g/8 oz potatoes, peeled and sliced**

**pinch of sugar**

**2–3 tablespoons mild curry powder**

**½ teaspoon powdered cumin**

**½ teaspoon turmeric**

**150 ml/¼ pint double cream**

**salt and pepper**

# Chilled Carrot Vichyssoise

**1** Melt the butter or margarine in a saucepan and cook the onion until soft but not golden. Add the carrots and leeks and cook over a moderate heat for 2–3 minutes, stirring constantly. Add 600 ml/1 pint water, the stock and coriander. Stir in salt to taste.

**2** Bring the mixture to the boil, then lower the heat, cover the pan and simmer for 30–35 minutes, or until the vegetables are tender. Cool slightly.

**3** In a blender or food processor purée the mixture in batches until smooth. Transfer each successive batch to a bowl, cover closely and chill in the refrigerator for at least 3 hours. Just before serving stir in the chilled cream. Serve in chilled soup bowls and sprinkle each serving with finely chopped parsley or coriander.

- Serves 6–8
- Preparation time: about 15 minutes, plus 3 hours chilling time
- Cooking time: 35 minutes

**50 g/2 oz butter or margarine**

**1 onion, chopped**

**500 g/1 lb carrots, sliced**

**375 g/12 oz leeks, white parts only, trimmed, cleaned and sliced**

**600 ml/1 pint Vegetable Stock (see page 122)**

**1 teaspoon chopped fresh coriander or ½ teaspoon dried leaf coriander**

**150 ml/¼ pint double cream, chilled**

**salt and pepper**

**finely chopped fresh parsley or coriander leaves, to garnish**

# Cauliflower Soup

Cauliflower is a versatile vegetable that can be transformed into a variety of flavoursome soups. This variation is illustrated opposite.

**1** Melt the butter or margarine in a large saucepan and add the onion, celery and cauliflower. Cook covered, for 5–8 minutes over a moderate heat. Stir frequently. Stir in the stock with 450 ml/¾ pint of the milk. Bring the mixture to the boil, then lower the heat and simmer, covered, for 25 minutes.

**2** In a blender or food processor purée the mixture in batches until smooth, transferring each successive batch to a clean saucepan. Stir in 300 ml/½ pint of the remaining milk. Add salt and pepper to taste and stir in the nutmeg.

**3** In a small bowl dissolve the cornflour in the remaining milk, add it to the cauliflower mixture. Stir constantly and bring to the boil. Lower the heat and simmer for 2 minutes. Serve at once in heated soup bowls or plates. Garnish each portion with a sprinkling of finely chopped parsley.

*50 g/2 oz butter or margarine*

*1 onion, chopped*

*1 celery stick, sliced*

*1 large cauliflower, about 750 g/1½ lb, cut into small florets*

*900 ml/1½ pints Vegetable Stock (see page 122)*

*600 ml/1 pint milk*

*1 teaspoon grated nutmeg*

*1 tablespoon cornflour*

*salt and white pepper*

*finely chopped fresh parsley, to garnish*

- Serves 6–8
- Preparation time: 15 minutes
- Cooking time: about 35 minutes

Variation

# Cauliflower Soup with Stilton

Follow the main recipe. At the end of the cooking time crumble in 250 g/8 oz Stilton and stir in 125 ml/4 fl oz double cream. Heat thoroughly, stirring all the time, but do not allow the soup to boil.

- Serves 6–8
- Preparation time: 15 minutes
- Cooking time: 35 minutes

Variation

# Curried Cream of Cauliflower Soup

Follow the main recipe, but stir the curry powder and turmeric into the onion, celery and cauliflower mixture and cook it in the butter or margarine for 5–8 minutes before adding the stock and the milk. Add the cream at the end of the cooking time and heat thoroughly without boiling. Garnish with a sprinkling of finely chopped green spring onion tops or snipped chives.

- Serves 6-8
- Preparation time: 15 minutes
- Cooking time: 35 minutes

**50 g/2 oz butter or margarine**

**I onion, chopped**

**I celery stick, sliced**

**I large cauliflower, about 750 g/1½ lb, cut into small florets**

**I tablespoon curry powder**

**½ teaspoon turmeric**

**900 ml/1½ pints Vegetable Stock (see page 122)**

**150 ml/¼ pint milk**

**I teaspoon grated nutmeg**

**I tablespoon cornflour**

**150 ml/¼ pint double cream**

**salt and pepper**

**finely chopped green onion tops or snipped chives, to garnish**

# Aubergine Soup

The other name of this unique vegetable is 'eggplant' as these fruiting vegetables grew to the size and shape of eggs in their native East Indies when first discovered.

**1** In a large heavy-bottomed saucepan heat the olive oil and sweat the onion, carrot, celery, garlic and aubergine. Cover with a tight-fitting lid and cook over a low heat, stirring frequently, for about 15–18 minutes, or until all the vegetables are softened.

**2** Add the stock, bring the mixture to the boil and simmer, covered, for 1 hour, or until the vegetables are very soft. Add the fresh basil to the mixture and cool slightly.

**3** In a blender or food processor purée the mixture in batches until it is very smooth, transferring each successive batch to a clean saucepan.

**4** Stir in the Parmesan, sherry and cream. Reheat gently without boiling. Season the soup with a little salt and pepper before serving.

*3 tablespoons olive oil*

*1 onion, chopped*

*1 carrot, chopped*

*2 celery sticks, sliced*

*1 garlic clove, chopped*

*750 g/1½ lb peeled and chopped aubergine*

*1.2 litres/2 pints Vegetable Stock (see page 122)*

*2 tablespoons coarsely chopped fresh basil*

*2 tablespoons grated Parmesan cheese*

*1 tablespoon medium dry sherry*

*125 ml/4 fl oz double cream*

*salt and black pepper*

- Serves 4–6
- Preparation time: 25 minutes
- Cooking time: about 1¼ hours

## Variation

# *Grilled Aubergine Soup*

First halve the aubergines lengthways. Cook under a pre-heated grill until charred and softened. Cool slightly then remove any charred patches, from the aubergines and chop them roughly. Proceed as in the main recipe.

- Serves 4–6
- Preparation time: 30 minutes
- Cooking time: 1¼ hours

# Kale Soup with Garlic Croûtons

Garlic croûtons provide a crisp, tasty counterpoint to the kale soup, illustrated opposite. The croûtons can be made in advance and kept in an airtight container in the refrigerator. To reheat the croûtons spread them on a baking sheet and place in a very hot oven for a few minutes.

**1** Melt the butter or margarine in a large saucepan and cook the onion over a moderate heat until soft but not brown. Stir frequently. Add the carrots and kale in batches, stirring all the time. Cook for 2 minutes. Add 1.2 litres/2 pints water, the stock, lemon juice, potatoes and nutmeg, with salt and pepper to taste. Bring to the boil, stirring from time to time. Lower the heat, cover and simmer for 30–35 minutes or until all the vegetables are soft.

**2** In a blender or food processor purée the mixture in batches, transferring each succesive batch to a clean pan. If it is too thick add some water.

**3** To prepare the croûtons. Cut the bread into 1 cm/½ inch squares. Heat the oil in a large frying pan, add the garlic and cook over a moderate heat for 1 minute. Add the bread squares and fry, turning frequently, until evenly golden brown. Using a slotted spoon transfer the garlic croûtons to kitchen paper to drain. Discard the garlic. Add the thinly shredded kale to the pan and fry, stirring constantly until crispy.

**4** To serve the soup, check the seasoning and reheat without boiling. Serve in heated soup plates with the garlic croûtons.

*50 g/2 oz butter or margarine*

*1 onion, chopped*

*2 carrots, sliced*

*500 g/1 lb kale, thick stems removed and discarded*

*600 ml/1 pint Vegetable Stock (see page 122)*

*1 tablespoon lemon juice*

*300 g/10 oz potatoes, peeled and sliced*

*pinch of grated nutmeg*

*salt and pepper*

*2 kale leaves, thinly shredded, to garnish*

*For the croûtons:*

*6–8 slices of white or brown bread, crusts removed*

*6–8 tablespoons olive oil*

*3 garlic cloves, sliced*

- Serves 8–10
- Preparation time: 20–25 minutes
- Cooking time: about 40 minutes

# Courgette Soup with Fresh Ginger

Fresh root ginger, so popular in Oriental cooking, livens up the slight blandness of the courgette.

**1** Wash the courgettes, cut off the ends and slice thickly into a colander. Sprinkle with salt and leave to stand for 10–15 minutes. Rinse under cold running water, drain thoroughly and pat dry with kitchen paper.

**2** Melt the butter or margarine in a pan and cook the onions over a moderate heat until soft but not golden. Add the courgettes and cook over a low heat for 5 minutes. Stir frequently.

**3** Add the stock, ginger and nutmeg to the pan with pepper to taste. Bring the mixture to the boil, add the potatoes and lower the heat. Simmer, partially covered, for 40–45 minutes, or until the vegetables are very soft.

**4** In a blender or food processor purée the mixture in batches until smooth, transferring each successive batch to a clean saucepan. Reheat gently. Serve in heated soup bowls. Garnish each portion with a swirl of cream.

*1.5 kg/3 lb small courgettes*
*50 g/2 oz butter or margarine*
*250 g/8 oz onions, chopped*
*1 litre/1¾ pints Vegetable Stock (see page 122)*
*1 tablespoon grated fresh root ginger*
*pinch of grated nutmeg*
*375 g/12 oz potatoes, peeled and chopped*
*salt and pepper*
*150 ml/¼ pint single cream, to garnish*

- Serves 6
- Preparation time: 15 minutes
- Cooking time: 55 minutes

## Variation

# Chilled Courgette Soup

This soup can be served cold. Chill the cream. Pour the puréed soup into a bowl. When cool, cover it closely and chill in the refrigerator for at least 3 hours. Serve in chilled bowls. Garnish each portion with a swirl of chilled cream.

- Serves 6
- Preparation time: 15 minutes, plus 3 hours chilling time
- Cooking time: 55 minutes

# Yellow Pepper Soup

Slightly sweet, yellow peppers are milder in flavour than green ones. All peppers are rich in Vitamin C.

**1** Core and deseed the peppers. Chop 1 pepper half finely and place it in a small saucepan. Chop the remaining peppers roughly.

**2** Melt 50 g/2 oz of the butter or margarine in another saucepan and cook the onion and roughly chopped peppers for 5 minutes. Stir frequently. Stir in the stock, curry powder, turmeric and coriander, then add the potatoes. Bring to the boil, then lower the heat and simmer, partially covered, for 40–45 minutes, or until the vegetables are very soft.

**3** Melt the remaining butter with the finely chopped pepper in the small pan. Cook over a gentle heat until the pepper is very soft. Set aside for the garnish.

**4** In a blender or food processor purée the onion, pepper and potato mixture in batches until very smooth, transferring each successive batch to a clean saucepan. Reheat gently. Serve in heated soup plates or bowls. Garnish each portion with a little of the sautéed chopped pepper.

- Serves 4–6
- Preparation time: 15–20 minutes
- Cooking time: 50–55 minutes

*3 yellow peppers*

*75 g/3 oz butter or margarine*

*1 small onion, chopped*

*1.2 litres/2 pints Vegetable Stock (see page 122)*

*1 teaspoon mild curry powder*

*¼ teaspoon turmeric*

*1 tablespoon chopped fresh coriander, or 1 teaspoon dried leaf coriander*

*300 g/10 oz potatoes, peeled and chopped*

*salt*

# Red Pepper and Potato Soup

**1** Heat the olive oil in a large saucepan. Add the garlic, onion and peppers and fry for 5 minutes, stirring frequently.

**2** Add the vegetable stock, rosemary, sugar and tomato purée. Stir well, then add the potatoes. Bring the mixture to the boil, lower the heat and simmer, partially covered, for 40–45 minutes, or until the vegetables are very soft.

**3** In a blender or food processor, purée the mixture in batches until it is very smooth, transferring each successive batch to a clean saucepan. Season with salt and pepper. Reheat gently and serve in heated soup bowls or plates.

- Serves 4–6
- Preparation time: 15 minutes
- Cooking time: about 50 minutes

*3 tablespoons olive oil*

*1 garlic clove, chopped*

*1 onion, chopped*

*2 red peppers, cored, deseeded and chopped*

*1.2 litres/2 pints Vegetable Stock (see page 122)*

*½ teaspoon finely chopped fresh rosemary, or ¼ teaspoon dried rosemary*

*¼ teaspoon sugar*

*2 tablespoons tomato purée*

*250 g/8 oz potatoes, peeled and chopped*

*salt and pepper*

**69**

# Fish Soups

The range of fish soup recipes here is vast, you can choose from a hearty Bouillabaisse that is so full of ingredients that it is a meal in itself or a delicate luxurious soup such as Chilled Cream of Smoked Salmon Soup which would make an excellent dinner party starter. When using these recipes experiment with different types of fish and try to use vegetables and herbs in season.

# Prawn Soup with Okra

Okra, also known as 'ladies' fingers', gives a satin smoothness and an unusual flavour to this soup, illustrated on pages 70-71.

**I** Melt the butter or margarine in a saucepan and then add the onion and celery. Cover the pan and cook over a moderate heat until the onion starts to soften, but has not browned at all. Add both the stock and the rice to the pan. Cook over a low heat, covered, for 20 minutes or until the rice is tender.

**2** Prepare the okra by cutting away the conical cap from the stalk end, then cut the okra into 1 cm/½ inch slices.

**3** Add the tomatoes, okra, prawns and ham to the soup and cook, uncovered, for a further 5–8 minutes, stirring frequently during the cooking time. Serve the soup in heated bowls, garnished generously with the small parsley leaves.

*50 g/2 oz butter or margarine*

*I onion, chopped finely*

*200 g/7 oz celery, sliced finely*

*I litre/1¾ pints Fish Stock (see page 121)*

*50 g/2 oz long-grain white rice*

*250 g/8 oz okra*

*2 tomatoes, skinned (see page 9) and chopped finely*

*250 g/8 oz cooked peeled prawns, thawed if frozen*

*50 g/2 oz cooked ham, cut into fine strips*

*small parsley leaves, to garnish*

- Serves 4–6
- Preparation time: 15 minutes
- Cooking time: 30–35 minutes

# Chilled Prawn and Yogurt Soup

This tangy refreshing soup needs no cooking, but the herbs have to be fresh.

**I** Peel the cucumber. Cut it in half, remove the seeds, then cut all the flesh into small dice. Place in a sieve or colander, sprinkle with salt and leave to drain for 20 minutes. Rinse under cold running water, drain the cucumber and squeeze dry with kitchen paper.

**2** In a blender or food processor blend the yogurt, soured cream, milk, sugar, pepper and Tabasco sauce with salt to taste. Pour the blended mixture into a bowl.

**3** Stir in the prawns, mint, chives and dill, then add the cucumber. Mix well, cover closely and chill in the refrigerator for at least 2 hours.

**4** Serve the soup in chilled bowls, garnishing each portion with a sprig of mint and a dusting of paprika.

*I large cucumber*

*150 ml/¼ pint natural yogurt*

*150 ml/¼ pint soured cream*

*125 ml/4 fl oz milk*

*¼ teaspoon caster sugar*

*¼ teaspoon white pepper*

*¼ teaspoon Tabasco sauce*

*200 g/7 oz cooked peeled prawns, thawed if frozen*

*I tablespoon finely chopped fresh mint*

*I tablespoon snipped fresh chives*

*I tablespoon snipped fresh dill*

*salt*

*To garnish:*

*4 small sprigs of mint*

*paprika*

- Serves 4
- Preparation time: 10 minutes, plus at least 2 hours chilling time

# Prawn Gumbo

This Cajun 'gumbo' is traditional to the Louisiana coast of the US. 'Gumbo' can be made with a variety of vegetables, meats and seafood, but okra is its most important ingredient. The soup can be made 24 hours in advance and kept, covered, in the refrigerator.

1 Bring a large saucepan of lightly salted water to the boil. Add the rice and cook for 8–10 minutes, or until tender. Drain the rice and set aside.

2 Melt the butter in a large heavy-bottomed saucepan. Add the garlic and onion and cook gently for about 5 minutes, or until soft and slightly golden. Add the red pepper and cook over a moderate heat for a further 5 minutes, stirring constantly. Stir in the tomatoes and cayenne and mix well. Pour in the fish stock and bring the mixture to the boil. Add the okra, lower the heat, cover the pan and cook for 20 minutes, stirring occasionally.

3 Add the prawns, rice and lime juice to the soup. Stir well, cover, and simmer for a further 5–8 minutes. Season with salt and pepper and add a little more cayenne if liked.

*50 g/2 oz long-grain white rice*

*50 g/2 oz butter*

*2 garlic cloves, crushed*

*1 onion, chopped*

*1 red pepper, cored, deseeded and chopped finely*

*4 ripe tomatoes, skinned (see page 9) and chopped*

*¼ teaspoon cayenne pepper, or more to taste*

*1.2 litres/2 pints Fish Stock (see page 121)*

*375 g/12 oz okra, trimmed and sliced*

*375 g/12 oz cooked, peeled prawns, thawed if frozen, dried on kitchen paper*

*1 tablespoon freshly squeezed lime juice*

*salt and pepper*

- Serves 4–6
- Preparation time: 20 minutes
- Cooking time: 30 minutes

# Simple Prawn Bisque

1 Melt the butter or margarine in a large saucepan and add the onion, carrot and celery. Cook for 5 minutes over a moderate heat, or until the vegetables begin to soften. Stir constantly.

2 Set aside 125 g/4 oz of the prawns. Add the remaining prawns to the pan with the chopped tomatoes, stock, sherry, bay leaf, nutmeg and potatoes. Stir in pepper to taste. Bring the mixture to simmering point, then reduce the heat further and cook, covered, for 25–30 minutes, or until all the vegetables are very tender. Remove the bay leaf.

3 In a blender or food processor purée the mixture in batches, transferring each successive batch to a clean saucepan. Add the reserved prawns, salt to taste and reheat. Just before serving stir in the cream. Sprinkle the soup with finely chopped parsley or chives.

*50 g/2 oz butter or margarine*

*1 small onion, chopped finely*

*1 carrot, chopped finely*

*1 celery stick, sliced finely*

*500 g/1 lb cooked, peeled prawns, thawed if frozen*

*1 x 397 g/14 oz can chopped tomatoes*

*900 ml/1½ pints Fish Stock (see page 121)*

*1 tablespoon medium dry sherry*

*1 bay leaf*

*pinch of ground nutmeg*

*250 g/8 oz potatoes, peeled and sliced finely*

*125 ml/4 fl oz double cream*

*salt and pepper*

*1 tablespoon finely chopped fresh parsley or snipped chives, to garnish*

- Serves 6
- Preparation time: about 15 minutes
- Cooking time: 35–40 minutes

# Crab and Rice Soup

This tasty crab soup is illustrated opposite.

**1** Cut the crab meat into 1 cm/½ inch pieces. Heat the oil in a heavy-bottomed saucepan and sauté the crab meat until lightly browned. Add the onion and cook over a moderate heat for 5 minutes, stirring constantly. Add the tomatoes, paprika, salt and 1.8 litres/3 pints boiling water. Cover the pan and cook over a low heat, for about 45 minutes.

**2** Meanwhile pound the garlic cloves in a mortar with a pinch of salt and the sprigs of parsley. Add the saffron strands and 2 tablespoons of the simmering stock. Stir the mixture well.

**3** Add the rice and the garlic mixture to the saucepan. Simmer, partially covered, for 20 minutes or until the rice is tender. Turn off the heat and leave the soup to rest on the stove for 2–3 minutes Stir and adjust the seasoning if necessary. Pour the soup into a heated tureen and serve hot with croûtons, if using.

- Serves 6
- Preparation time: 15 minutes
- Cooking time: 1¼ hours

**500 g/1 lb white crab meat**

**4 tablespoons olive oil**

**1 onion, chopped**

**250 g/8 oz tomatoes, skinned (see page 9) and chopped**

**1 teaspoon paprika**

**½ teaspoon salt, or to taste**

**2 garlic cloves**

**2 sprigs of parsley, leaves stripped from stems**

**3 saffron strands**

**250 g/8 oz long-grain white rice**

**salt**

**croûtons, to garnish (see page 66, optional)**

# Prawn and Fennel Soup

1 Melt the butter or margarine in a saucepan. Add the fennel, cover the pan tightly and cook over a moderate heat for 5 minutes, or until it begins to soften. Stir from time to time.

2 Add the stock, milk, pepper and potatoes and bring the mixture to simmering point. Cook, covered, over a low heat for 15–20 minutes, or until the vegetables are soft.

3 In a blender of food processor purée the mixture in batches until smooth, transferring each successive batch to a clean saucepan. Add the prawns, season with salt and stir in the cream. Reheat the soup over a low heat. Serve in heated soup plates or bowls. Finally, garnish each portion of soup with a sprinkling of finely chopped fennel leaves.

- Serves 4–6
- Preparation time: 10–15 minutes
- Cooking time: about 25 minutes

*50 g/2 oz butter or margarine*

*2 fennel bulbs, sliced finely, leaves reserved to garnish*

*600 ml/1 pint Fish Stock (see page 121)*

*600 ml/1 pint milk*

*¼ teaspoon white pepper*

*300 g/10 oz potatoes, peeled and chopped*

*175 g/9 oz cooked peeled prawns, peeled and thawed if frozen*

*salt*

*150 ml/¼ pint single cream*

# Mussel Chowder

Use the small plump European mussels – the large New Zealand mussels are not suitable for this chowder.

1 Heat the olive oil in a heavy-bottomed saucepan and cook the bacon, uncovered, over a moderate heat until browned. Add the onions, celery and pepper and cook for 5 minutes or until the vegetables soften. Stir frequently. Add the fish stock, potatoes, bay leaf and marjoram. Bring to the boil, then lower the heat, cover the pan and simmer for 15–20 minutes, or until the potatoes are tender.

2 In a small bowl blend the flour with 150 ml/¼ pint of the milk. Whisk the mixture into the chowder, stir until it begins to boil, then slowly add the remaining milk. Add salt and pepper to taste.

3 Lower the heat, add the mussels and simmer gently for 5 minutes, stirring from time to time. Do not allow the chowder to boil. Stir in the cream and pour the chowder into a heated soup tureen. Sprinkle the parsley over the top to garnish and serve the soup with crusty French bread.

*2 tablespoons olive oil*

*250 g/8 oz of rindless smoked streaky bacon, chopped*

*2 onions, chopped finely*

*1 celery stick, sliced finely*

*1 green pepper, cored, deseeded and finely chopped*

*450 ml/¾ pint Fish Stock (see page 121)*

*250 g/8 oz potatoes, peeled and diced*

*1 bay leaf*

*½ teaspoon chopped fresh marjoram leaves, or ¼ teaspoon dried marjoram*

*3 tablespoons plain white flour*

*300 ml/½ pint milk*

*500 g/1 lb cooked shelled mussels, thawed if frozen*

*150 ml/¼ pint single cream*

*salt and white pepper*

*1 tablespoon finely chopped parsley, to garnish*

- Serves 4-6
- Preparation time: 10-15 minutes
- Cooking time: about 30 minutes

# Fish Soup with Rice and Tomatoes

**1** Rinse the fish under cold running water. Drain well. Cut it into 5cm/2 inch pieces. Place the fish in a colander and sprinkle with 1 teaspoon of salt. Set aside.

**2** Place all the vegetables with the parsley and fish head in a large saucepan. Add 1.8 litres/3 pints water, with a little salt and pepper to taste. Cook over a moderate heat until the mixture boils, then lower the heat and simmer for about 45 minutes. Remove and discard the fish head and the parsley.

**3** Rinse the fish pieces again under cold running water and add them to the saucepan. Cook over a moderate heat, uncovered, for 15–20 minutes, or until the fish is cooked but still firm. Using a slotted spoon, remove the fish pieces from the saucepan and keep them hot in a covered dish. Slowly pour the olive oil into the soup, then add the rice. Cook over a moderate heat, partially covered, for 25 minutes or until the rice is tender. Return the fish pieces to the soup and reheat gently. Taste and adjust the seasoning if necessary and serve at once in heated bowls.

*750 g/1½ lb cod or haddock, skinned and boned*

*4 large tomatoes, skinned (see page 9) and chopped coarsely*

*2 large onions, sliced thinly*

*2 celery sticks, sliced thinly*

*4 sprigs of parsley*

*1 fish head*

*5 tablespoons olive oil*

*50 g/2 oz short-grain white rice*

*salt and pepper*

- Serves 4–6
- Preparation time: 15–20 minutes
- Cooking time: about 1½ hours

## Variation

# Haddock Soup with Rice and Tomatoes

Follow the main recipe but use 750 g/1½ lb haddock instead of the cod. Any other firm white fish such as coley, hake or whiting can be substituted for the cod, or why not try a mixture of firm white fish.

- Serves 4–6
- Preparation time: 15–20 minutes
- Cooking time: about 1½ hours

# Kipper Soup

The smoky flavour and bright colour of the kipper make this soup, illustrated opposite, truly original.

**1** Place the fish in a wide saucepan and add 600 ml/1 pint water. Bring to simmering point, then lower the heat further, cover the pan tightly and cook for 5 minutes. Drain the fish, reserving 450 ml/¾ pint of the liquid in a jug.

**2** Skin and flake the fish. In a blender or food processor blend the fish with the tomatoes, tomato purée and 300 ml/½ pint of the reserved cooking liquid. Return the mixture to the clean pan.

**3** In a small bowl mix the cornflour to a cream with the remaining cooking liquid. Stir the mixture into the pan and add the lemon juice, Worcestershire sauce and celery salt, with cayenne to taste. Stir and simmer for 5–8 minutes, or until the soup thickens slightly. Serve in heated soup bowls. Garnish each portion with a swirl of soured cream, if liked, and a generous sprinkling of snipped chives.

*375 g/12 oz kipper fillet*

*2 x 397 g/14 oz cans plum tomatoes*

*1 tablespoon tomato purée*

*1½ tablespoons cornflour*

*1 teaspoon lemon juice*

*1 tablespoon Worcestershire sauce*

*¼ teaspoon celery salt*

*cayenne pepper*

*To garnish:*

*3 tablespoons soured cream (optional)*

*2 tablespoons snipped fresh chives*

- Serves 6
- Preparation time: 10–15 minutes
- Cooking time: 15–20 minutes

# Chilled Cream of Smoked Salmon Soup

A soup designed to impress: a rich, luxurious starter!

**1** Melt the butter in a saucepan and cook the onion and garlic over a moderate heat, stirring constantly, for 1 minute. Add the salmon and cook, stirring, for 1 minute more. Sprinkle the flour over the mixture and stir. Cook for 30 seconds, then slowly pour in the stock, stirring all the time. Bring the mixture to the boil, stirring constantly. Lower the heat and simmer the soup, uncovered, for 5 minutes.

**2** Add the lemon juice, bay leaf and paprika with salt and pepper to taste. Simmer, uncovered, for 5–8 minutes, then remove the saucepan from the heat and let the mixture cool. Remove the bay leaf.

**3** In a blender or food processor purée the mixture in batches, straining each successive batch through a coarse sieve into a bowl. Stir in the cream, prawns and snipped dill. Chill the soup, closely covered for 3–4 hours or overnight. Serve in chilled bowls, garnishing each portion with a sprig of dill.

*50 g/2 oz butter*

*1 onion, chopped*

*1 garlic clove, finely chopped*

*250 g/8 oz smoked salmon, chopped finely*

*3 tablespoons plain flour*

*900 ml/1½ pints Chicken Stock (see page 121)*

*1 tablespoon lemon juice*

*1 bay leaf*

*¼ teaspoon paprika*

*150 ml/¼ pint single cream*

*125 g/4 oz cooked peeled prawns, thawed if frozen*

*1 teaspoon fresh dill, snipped*

*salt and white pepper*

*6 sprigs of fresh dill, to garnish*

- Serves 6
- Preparation time: about 15 minutes, plus 3–4 hours or overnight chilling
- Cooking time: about 15 minutes

# Tuna and Red Pepper Chowder

**1** Melt the butter or margarine in a saucepan. Add the pepper and celery, cover the pan and cook for 8–10 minutes, stirring frequently. When the mixture gets a little dry, moisten it with the white wine.

**2** Add the fish stock, potatoes and marjoram and cook, partially covered, for 15 minutes over a moderate heat.

**3** Stir in the sweetcorn and tuna, season with salt and pepper to taste and cook, uncovered, over a low heat for a further 10 minutes. Stir in the parsley. Serve the chowder in heated bowls, with crusty French bread, if liked.

*50 g/2 oz butter or margarine*

*1 small red pepper, cored, deseeded and chopped*

*1 celery stick, sliced finely*

*1 tablespoon dry white wine*

*1.2 litres/2 pints Fish Stock (see page 121)*

*250 g/8 oz potatoes, peeled and cut into 1 cm/½ inch dice*

*1 teaspoon finely chopped fresh marjoram, or ½ teaspoon dried marjoram*

*1 x 340 g/11½ oz can sweetcorn, drained*

*1 x 185 g/6½ oz tuna chunks in brine, drained and shredded*

*2 tablespoons finely chopped parsley*

*salt and pepper*

- Serves 4–6
- Preparation time: 10–12 minutes
- Cooking time: 35 minutes

# Bouillabaisse

Originally Bouillabaisse was not intended to be a soup but a fish stew. Today there are countless different variations for this classic French soup.

**1** Heat the oil in a large heavy-bottomed saucepan. Add the garlic and onions and cook, covered, for 3–5 minutes, or until the onions are transparent but not brown. Add the mackerel, whiting, haddock or cod and cook, uncovered, over a moderate heat for 10 minutes. Stir from time to time.

**2** Add the prawns and tomatoes. Dissolve the saffron strands in the hot fish stock and add to the pan with the bay leaf, parsley, and salt and pepper to taste. Stir and bring the mixture to the boil. Lower the heat and simmer, covered, for 15 minutes, then add the mussels and continue cooking for a further 10 minutes or until the fish is cooked.

**3** Discard the bay leaf and parsley sprigs and discard any mussels that have not opened. Place the bread in a warmed soup tureen and ladle in the soup. Sprinkle with the chopped parsley before serving.

- Serves 6–8
- Preparation time: about 35 minutes
- Cooking time: 30–35 minutes

*4 tablespoons olive oil*

*2 garlic cloves, chopped finely*

*2 onions, chopped*

*500 g/1 lb prepared mackerel, cut into chunks*

*500 g/1 lb whiting fillet, cut into chunks*

*500 g/1 lb haddock or cod fillet, cut into chunks*

*250 g/8 oz uncooked prawns, peeled*

*6 tomatoes, skinned (see page 9) and chopped*

*½ teaspoon saffron strands*

*1.5 litre/2½ pints hot Fish Stock (see page 121)*

*1 bay leaf*

*3 parsley sprigs*

*10-12 mussels, scrubbed and debearded*

*6-8 slices French bread*

*salt and pepper*

*2 tablespoons finely chopped fresh parsley, to garnish*

*Variation*

## Bouillabaisse with Crab Meat

Follow the main recipe but add 175 g/6 oz crab meat in step 2 with the prawns and the tomatoes. Continue as in the main recipe.

- Serves 6–8
- Preparation time: about 35 minutes
- Cooking time: 30–35 minutes

# Smoked Haddock Chowder

The chowder, now widely regarded as an American dish, stems from the French word 'chaudière' which relates to the cauldron or kettle in which French peasants had been cooking long before the discovery of America. The chowder is comfort food – it is homely and very versatile and can be prepared from shellfish, fish, potatoes and vegetables. This variation is illustrated opposite.

**1** Combine the potatoes, onion, bay leaf, marjoram and 600 ml/1 pint water in a saucepan. Bring the mixture to the boil, then lower the heat and simmer, covered, for 5 minutes.

**2** Add the haddock fillet, nutmeg and milk, with white pepper to taste. Simmer the soup, partially covered, for 20 minutes. Remove and discard the bay leaf.

**3** Serve the chowder in heated soup bowls. Sprinkle each portion with finely chopped marjoram, to garnish. Serve the croûtons separately, if using.

*500 g/1 lb potatoes, peeled and cut into 1 cm/½ inch cubes*

*1 onion, chopped finely*

*1 bay leaf*

*½ teaspoon chopped fresh marjoram, or ¼ teaspoon dried marjoram*

*500 g/1 lb skinned smoked haddock fillet, chopped coarsely with, any remaining bones removed*

*¼ teaspoon ground nutmeg*

*450 ml/¾ pint milk*

*white pepper*

*To garnish:*

*2 tablespoons finely chopped fresh marjoram*

*croûtons (see page 66, optional)*

- Serves 4–6
- Preparation time: 10–15 minutes
- Cooking time: 35 minutes

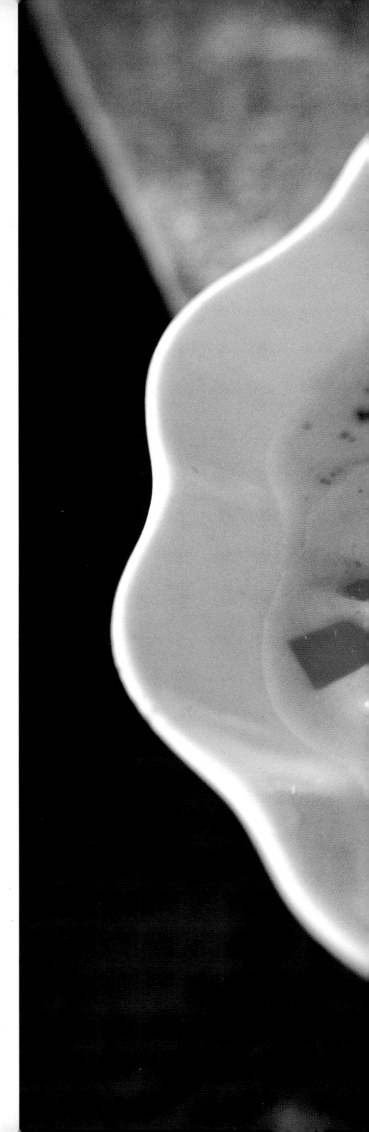

# SweetCorn and Smoked Haddock Chowder

**1** Combine the potato and bay leaf in a saucepan. Add the milk and 600 ml/1 pint water. Bring the mixture to the boil. Lower the heat and simmer, uncovered, for about 5 minutes, or until the diced potato is almost tender.

**2** Add the haddock fillet, cover and simmer for a further 10 minutes. Then add the sweetcorn and peas and cook over a moderate heat for 5 minutes more. Remove and discard the bay leaf.

**3** In a small bowl mix the cornflour, paprika and white pepper to a smooth cream with 3–4 tablespoons of the liquid from the saucepan. Add the cornflour mixture to the saucepan and cook, stirring constantly, for about 5 minutes or until the soup has thickened. Add salt if needed and stir in the parsley. Serve the chowder in heated soup bowls.

*1 large potato, peeled and diced*

*1 bay leaf*

*250–300 g/8–10 oz skinned smoked haddock fillet, chopped coarsely, with any remaining bones removed*

*1 x 200 g/7 oz can sweetcorn, drained*

*3 tablespoons frozen green peas*

*1½ tablespoons cornflour*

*¼ teaspoon paprika*

*½ teaspoon white pepper*

*salt (optional)*

*2 tablespoons finely chopped fresh parsley*

- Serves 4–6
- Preparation time: 10–15 minutes
- Cooking time: about 25 minutes

# Thai Hot and Sour Soup

This soup is only for those who like hot fiery food. The Thai chilli paste 'nam pla' is available from Thai grocers.

**1** Wash, peel and de-vein the prawns. Reserve the shells. Wash the prawns again, pat dry with kitchen paper and set aside in a covered bowl, in the refrigerator. Wearing rubber gloves, cut the chillies in half, removing the seeds, then chop the chillies very finely.

**2** In a large saucepan combine the prawn shells, lemon grass and lemon rind with the stock. Bring to the boil, lower the heat and simmer for 20 minutes.

**3** Strain the stock into a clean saucepan and add the salt, lime juice and chilli paste, or the chilli powder mixture. Bring the liquid to the boil, add the mushrooms and boil for about 1 minute, then drop in the prawns and cook for a further 2 minutes, or until the prawns turn opaque. Add more salt and lime juice, if liked.

**4** Ladle the soup into a heated tureen or serve in individual heated bowls. Garnish with finely chopped green chillies and coriander leaves.

*500 g/1 lb uncooked prawns in shells*

*2 hot green chillies or to taste*

*2 tablespoons dried lemon grass*

*1 tablespoon finely grated lemon rind*

*1.2 litres/2 pints Chicken Stock (see page 121)*

*¼ teaspoon salt, or to taste*

*3 tablespoons freshly squeezed lime juice, or to taste*

*1 teaspoon mild or medium hot Thai chilli paste, ('nam prik pow') or ¼ teaspoon chilli powder mixed with ¼ teaspoon sugar and ½ teaspoon vegetable oil*

*12 open cup mushrooms, quartered*

*To garnish:*

*2 fresh hot green chillies, or to taste, deseeded and chopped finely*

*3 tablespoons coriander leaves*

- Serves 6
- Preparation time: about 25 minutes
- Cooking time: 25–30 minutes

# Haddock and Fennel Soup

The slight aniseed flavour of fennel enhances most fish soups. Its feathery leaves (fronds) can be chopped finely and sprinkled over the soup as a garnish.

**1** Melt the butter or margarine in a saucepan. Add the fennel and leek slices and simmer for 5 minutes, or until soft. Add the stock, bay leaf and potatoes. Bring to the boil, then lower the heat and simmer, covered, for 10–15 minutes or until the vegetables are tender. Remove the bay leaf.

**2** In a separate saucepan combine the fish with the milk and white pepper. Bring to the boil, then lower the heat and simmer, covered, for 5 minutes. Leave to stand with the lid on for a further 5 minutes, then break the fish into large flakes.

**3** Purée 300 ml/½ pint of the fennel mixture in a blender or food processor until smooth. Return the purée to the saucepan and add the milk and fish mixture. Stir well and heat thoroughly without boiling. Serve in heated bowls, garnished with the reserved finely chopped fennel leaves.

*25 g/2 oz butter or margarine*

*250 g/8 oz fennel bulbs, sliced finely, leaves reserved for garnish*

*1 leek, white part only, trimmed, cleaned and sliced*

*600 ml/1 pint Fish Stock (see page 121)*

*1 bay leaf*

*300 g/10 oz potatoes, peeled, halved and finely sliced*

*250 g/8 oz skinned haddock fillet*

*300 ml/½ pint milk*

*½ teaspoon white pepper*

*salt*

- Serves 4–6
- Preparation time: 15 minutes
- Cooking time: 25–30 minutes

## *Variation*

# *Cod and Celery Soup*

This recipe makes an ideal alternative for people who do not like the aniseed taste of fennel.

Follow the main recipe but replace the haddock fillet with 250 g/8 oz skinned cod fillet and replace the fennel with 250 g/8 oz celery sticks, sliced thinly. Proceed as in the main recipe.

- Serves 4–6
- Preparation time: 10–15 minutes
- Cooking time: about 25 minutes

# Hearty Soups

The recipes in this chapter can easily be
served in place of a meal as
they are sustaining and full of nutritious
ingredients including beans,
pulses and filling vegetables. To make a
complete meal serve these soups
with a variety of breads such as French
bread, Italian Ciabatta, Soda Bread
or Garlic Bread.

# White Cabbage Soup with Meatballs

Cabbage, in all its varieties, is a favourite ingredient in European peasant soups. In this hearty, delicious dish the smooth, hard-packed white cabbage, also known as 'Dutch Cabbage', is the chief component.

**1** Discard the outer leaves and the centre core of the cabbage. Shred the cabbage coarsely.

**2** Melt the butter or margarine in a large, heavy-bottomed saucepan. Add the cabbage and sugar and cook, stirring constantly, until the cabbage is golden. Add the stock, allspice and peppercorns. Simmer the mixture, covered, for 30–35 minutes, or until the cabbage is tender. Add salt to taste.

**3** Make the meatballs. Place the breadcrumbs in a bowl, add 150 ml/¼ pint water and soak for 3 minutes. Add the veal, pork, egg yolks, salt, pepper, Worcestershire sauce and Dijon mustard. With a fork, stir the mixture vigorously until it is very smooth. Between the palms of your clean hands shape the mixture into balls the size of walnuts.

**4** Bring the soup to the boil and add the meatballs one by one. Lower the heat and simmer the soup, uncovered, for 10 minutes. Transfer the soup to a heated tureen and serve in large heated soup plates.

- Serves 4–6
- Preparation time: 25 minutes
- Cooking time: 45–50 minutes

*1 white cabbage (about 875 g/1¾ lb)*

*50 g/2 oz butter or margarine*

*2 teaspoons sugar*

*1.5 litres/2½ pints Beef Stock (see page 120)*

*3 allspice*

*6 white peppercorns*

*salt*

*Meatballs:*

*2 tablespoons dried white breadcrumbs*

*250 g/8 oz lean minced veal*

*250 g/8 oz lean minced pork*

*2 egg yolks*

*1 teaspoon salt*

*¼ teaspoon white pepper*

*1 teaspoon Worcestershire sauce*

*1 teaspoon Dijon mustard*

# Oxtail Soup

A cheap, nourishing soup. Thick and rich, it is almost a meal in itself.

**1** Melt the butter or lard in a heavy-bottomed saucepan. Add the oxtail and onions and cook over a moderate heat until lightly browned. Turn the oxtail pieces once.

**2** Add the celery, carrots, bay leaf, peppercorns, cloves and sugar, with salt and pepper to taste. Pour in 3 litres/5½ pints water. Bring the mixture to the boil, then lower the heat. Cover the pan and simmer for about 4 hours, or until the oxtail is tender.

**3** Using the oxtail pieces from the pan, strip the meat off the bones, shred and return the meat to the saucepan. Discard the bones.

**4** In a small basin mix the flour with enough milk to make a thin paste. Whisk it into the soup, stirring until the soup thickens. Add the wine or sherry and bring the soup slowly to the boil. Serve the soup hot in warmed soup plates. Garnish with finely chopped parsley.

- Serves 6-8
- Preparation time: about 20 minutes
- Cooking time: about 4¼ hours

*50 g/2 oz butter, lard or dripping*

*1 oxtail, about 900 g/2 lb, cut into 5 cm/2 inch pieces, excess fat removed*

*375 g/12 oz chopped onions*

*3 celery sticks, chopped*

*250 g/8 oz carrots, chopped*

*1 bay leaf, crushed*

*6 black peppercorns, crushed*

*2 cloves*

*¼ teaspoon sugar*

*1 tablespoon plain flour*

*milk, for mixing*

*150 ml/¼ pint red wine or 2 tablespoons dry sherry*

*salt and pepper*

*finely chopped fresh parsley, to garnish*

# Mulligatawny

The word 'mulligatawny' is a corruption of the Tamil words milagu-tuanni, which roughly means 'pepper water'. Later, during the British Raj, it was introduced by the Indian cooks and became known by its present name. It should be highly flavoured and very spicy.

**1** In a blender or food processor purée the onion, garlic and ginger with the cayenne, coriander, cumin and turmeric to a smooth paste, scraping down the sides of the jug or bowl with a wooden or plastic spatula from time to time.

**2** Heat the oil in a large heavy-bottomed saucepan and cook the onion paste over a moderate heat, stirring, for 2–3 minutes. Add the chicken breasts and cook, stirring, for a further 1–2 minutes.

**3** Slowly pour in the stock and 1.2 litres/2 pints water, stirring all the time. Add the rice and lentils. Simmer for 15–20 minutes, or until the rice is tender.

**4** Remove the chicken, cut it into small pieces and set aside. Purée 900 ml/1½ pints of the soup mixture in a blender or food processor, then return the purée to the remaining soup in the saucepan. Add a little water if the soup is too thick.

**5** Stir well, then add the lemon juice, coconut and reserved chicken pieces. Stir again and heat thoroughly without boiling for 3-5 minutes. Serve in heated bowls, garnishing each portion with a lemon slice.

- Serves 6–8
- Preparation time: 15–20 minutes
- Cooking time: 30–35 minutes

*1 onion, chopped*

*2 garlic cloves, chopped*

*2.5 cm/1 inch piece of fresh root ginger, peeled and chopped*

*¼ teaspoon cayenne pepper, or to taste*

*1 teaspoon ground coriander*

*½ teaspoon ground cumin*

*1 teaspoon ground turmeric*

*4 teaspoons vegetable oil*

*3 skinless, boneless chicken breasts, halved*

*1.2 litres/2 pints Chicken Stock (see page 122)*

*50 g/2 oz long-grain white rice*

*125 g/4 oz red lentils*

*1 tablespoon lemon juice*

*2 tablespoons grated creamed coconut*

*salt*

*6–8 lemon slices, to garnish*

# Barley Soup with Pork and Cabbage

**1** Heat the oil in a large, heavy-bottomed saucepan and cook the garlic and onion over a moderate heat until softened.

**2** Add the stock, 750 ml/1½ pints water, pork, carrots, cabbage and barley. Bring the mixture to the boil, then lower the heat, cover the pan and simmer for 20 minutes.

**3** Add the potatoes with salt and pepper to taste. If the soup is too thick, add a little water. Replace the lid and simmer for a further 30 minutes. Stir from time to time. Serve in heated soup bowls or plates.

- Serves 6
- Preparation time: 15 minutes
- Cooking time: 55 minutes

*4 tablespoons olive oil*

*1 garlic clove, chopped*

*1 onion, chopped*

*1.2 litres/2 pints Beef Stock (see page 120)*

*300 g/10 oz lean pork, cut into 2 cm/¾ inch strips*

*2 carrots, chopped*

*300 g/10 oz Spring or Savoy cabbage, trimmed and chopped coarsely*

*125 g/4 oz pearl barley*

*300 g/10 oz potatoes, peeled and cut into 1 cm/½ inch cubes*

*salt and pepper*

89

# Goulash Soup

Goulash stew and soup originated in Hungary and later became a very popular dish in Austria. Although there are several variations of Goulash Soup, illustrated opposite, the chief ingredients remain the paprika and caraway seeds which lend the soup its unmistakably aromatic flavour.

**1** Heat the oil in a heavy-bottomed saucepan and brown the meat in batches over a moderate heat. As each batch browns, transfer it to kitchen paper to drain. Cook the onions, garlic and celery in the remaining oil until transparent.
**2** Take the saucepan off the heat and stir in the paprika, caraway seeds, stock and 600 ml/1 pint water. Add the thyme, bay leaves, Tabasco and tomato purée. Stir well and add the cooked beef. Bring the mixture to the boil then lower the heat and simmer, partially covered, for 30 minutes.
**3** Add the diced potatoes and carrots and then simmer for a further 30 minutes, or until the potatoes are tender. Remove and discard all the bay leaves, if you wish. Serve the soup immediately in heated bowls or deep soup plates, garnishing each portion with a teaspoon of soured cream, if liked.

*3 tablespoons vegetable oil*

*750 g/1½ lb boneless lean beef, cut into 2.5 cm/1 inch strips*

*2 onions, chopped*

*2 garlic cloves, crushed*

*2 celery sticks, sliced*

*3 tablespoons paprika*

*1 tablespoon caraway seeds*

*1.2 litres/2 pints Beef Stock (see page 120)*

*¼ teaspoon dried thyme*

*2 bay leaves*

*¼ teaspoon Tabasco sauce, or to taste*

*3 tablespoons tomato purée*

*250 g/8 oz potatoes, peeled and cut into 1 cm/½ inch diced*

*3 carrots, cut into 1 cm/½ inch dice*

*6-8 teaspoons soured cream (optional)*

- Serves 6–8
- Preparation time: 10–15 minutes
- Cooking time: 1¼ hours

# Laksa

This soup from Singapore – a mixture of pork, noodles, vegetables, coconut and spices – is substantial enough to be served as a main course.

**1** Combine the pork fillet with 1.5 litres/2½ pints of the stock in a large saucepan. Add the soy sauce and sherry and bring the mixture to the boil, skimming off any scum that rises to the surface. Lower the heat and simmer, partially covered, for 20 minutes, or until the pork is just tender.

**2** Meanwhile heat the sesame and vegetable oil together in a second large saucepan. Add the ginger, garlic, coriander, turmeric and chilli powder. Stir well and fry gently over a moderate heat for about 5 minutes. Remove the pan from the heat.

**3** Remove the pork from the liquid and set aside. Add the noodles to the pan, return it to the heat and bring it back to the boil. Cover the pan tightly, immediately and remove it from the heat. Leave to stand for 5 minutes. Meanwhile cut the pork into thin 5 mm/¼ inch strips. Set aside.

**4** Drain the noodles, pouring the cooking liquid into the ginger and spice mixture. Stir well, add the creamed coconut and bring the mixture to the boil. Lower the heat, add the green pepper, spring onions, beans and carrots and simmer for about 8–10 minutes.

**5** Meanwhile cut the noodles into 5 cm/2 inch pieces with kitchen scissors. Add them to the soup together with the reserved pork and the bean sprouts. Add salt and pepper to taste. Bring the soup to the boil again and cook for 1-2 minutes. Serve the soup in heated bowls, with prawn crackers if liked.

*250 g/8 oz pork fillet*

*1.8 litres/3 pints Chicken Stock (see page 122)*

*3 tablespoons light soy sauce*

*2 tablespoons dry sherry*

*1 tablespoon sesame oil*

*1 tablespoon vegetable oil*

*5 cm/2 inch piece of fresh root ginger, cut into thin matchstick strips*

*2 garlic cloves, crushed*

*1¼ teaspoons ground coriander*

*1 teaspoon turmeric*

*¼ teaspoon chilli powder, or to taste*

*125 g/4 oz Chinese egg noodles*

*125 g/4 oz creamed coconut dissolved in 300 ml/½ pint boiling water*

*1 green pepper, cored, deseeded and cut into matchstick strips*

*5 spring onions, sliced*

*250 g/8 oz round green or French beans, trimmed and cut in half*

*2 carrots, cut into thin matchstick strips*

*125 g/4 oz fresh bean sprouts, washed*

*salt and pepper*

- Serves 4–6
- Preparation time: 10-15 minutes
- Cooking time: about 45 minutes

**92**

# Yellow Pea Soup with Chorizo

Chorizo is a spicy sausage originating from Spain and Latin America, made with pork and hot peppers. It gives the soup a special bite.

**I** Drain the split peas in a colander, rinse under cold running water and drain again.

**2** Heat the oil in a heavy-bottomed saucepan. Cook the sliced chorizo over a moderate heat, stirring, for 5 minutes. With a slotted spoon transfer the slices to kitchen paper to drain. Pour off all but 1 tablespoon of the fat in the pan.

**3** Add the onion and garlic to the pan and cook over a moderate heat until softened. Add the drained split peas, stock, 900 ml/1½ pints water, bay leaf and thyme. Bring the mixture to the boil, skimming off the froth as it rises to the surface. Lower the heat and simmer, partially covered, for 1¼ hours. Stir the mixture occasionally.

**4** Add the carrots and cook for a further 30 minutes, or until tender. Season with salt. Discard the bay leaf, add the reserved chorizo and cook for a further 10 minutes. Serve in heated deep soup bowls or plates.

*375 g/12 oz split yellow peas, soaked overnight in water to cover*

*2 tablespoons olive oil*

*3 chorizo, sliced thinly*

*1 onion, chopped*

*2 garlic cloves, chopped finely*

*1.2 litres/2 pints Chicken Stock (see page 122)*

*900 ml/1½ pints water*

*1 bay leaf*

*1 sprig of thyme, or ¼ teaspoon dried thyme*

*3 carrots, quartered lengthways and sliced thinly*

*salt*

- Serves 6-8
- Preparation time: 15–20 minutes, plus 6–12 hours soaking
- Cooking time: about 2 hours

# Spicy Chilli Bean Soup

**I** Drain the beans and rinse thoroughly under cold running water, then drain again.

**2** Heat the oil in a heavy-bottomed saucepan. Cook the sausage slices for 3–5 minutes over moderate heat. Stir constantly. With a slotted spoon remove the slices from the pan and drain on kitchen paper.

**3** Add the onion to the mixture of oil and sausage fat remaining in the pan and cook until softened. Stir frequently. Add the chilli powder, cumin and thyme. Cook the mixture, stirring, for 1 minute, then add the pinto beans, bay leaf and the chicken stock. Simmer, covered, for 1 hour.

*250 g/8 oz pinto beans, soaked overnight in water to cover*

*2 tablespoons olive oil*

*4 small or 2 large Kabanos sausages, sliced thinly*

*1 onion, chopped*

*1 tablespoon mild chilli powder, or to taste*

*1 teaspoon ground cumin*

*¼ teaspoon dried thyme*

*1 bay leaf*

*1.2 litres/2 pints Chicken Stock (see page 122)*

*2 garlic cloves, crushed*

*1 large red pepper, cored, deseeded and chopped*

*1 x 397g/14 oz can chopped tomatoes*

*salt*

**4** Add the garlic, red pepper and tomatoes. Simmer for a further hour, stirring from time to time. Add the sausages with salt to taste. Cook for a further 5 minutes, stirring frequently. Serve in heated deep soup bowls or plates.

- Serves 4–6
- Preparation time: 15 minutes, plus 8–12 hours soaking
- Cooking time: 2¼ hours

# Spanish Chickpea Soup

Known as 'garbanzo' in Spain, 'ceci' in Italy and 'chana dal' in India, the chickpea – a staple diet of the Middle East – is used in many European dishes, particularly stews and thick soups like this one illustrated opposite.

**1** Drain the chickpeas in a colander, rinse under cold running water and drain again. Put the bacon joint in a deep saucepan and cover with cold water. Bring the water briefly to the boil, then drain, discarding the water.

**2** Return the bacon joint to the clean saucepan. Add the chickpeas, onion, garlic, bay leaf, thyme, marjoram, parsley and 1.8 litres/3 pints water. Bring the mixture to the boil then lower the heat and simmer, partially covered, for 1½ hours. Remove and discard the onion, bay leaf and sprigs of thyme, marjoram and parsley. Lift out the hock, place it on a board and cut it into small pieces. Set the pieces aside.

**3** Add the stock, potatoes and cabbage to the pan and simmer for a further 30 minutes. Add the reserved hock pieces to the soup and cook for 10 minutes more. Season with salt and pepper to taste. Serve in heated soup plates.

*150 g/5 oz dried chickpeas, soaked for 48 hours in cold water to cover or 12 hours if covered with boiling water*

*1 small or ½ smoked, boneless bacon hock joint, about 500-750 g/1-1½ lb*

*1 onion, studded with 4 cloves*

*2 garlic cloves, crushed*

*1 bay leaf*

*1 sprig of thyme, or ¼ teaspoon dried thyme*

*1 sprig of marjoram, or ½ teaspoon dried marjoram*

*1 sprig of parsley*

*1.8 litres/3 pints Chicken Stock (see page 122)*

*300–375 g/10–12 oz potatoes, peeled and cut into 1 cm/½ inch cubes*

*300 g/10 oz Savoy cabbage, shredded*

*salt and pepper*

- Serves 8–10
- Preparation time: 15 minutes, plus 12–48 hours soaking
- Cooking time: 2½–2¾ hours

# Green Lentil and Bacon Soup

Also referred to as Continental lentils, these are, as the name suggests – popular in European cooking, and provide a wholesome soup which is a good source of protein. Unlike the orange and brown Indian lentils which quickly cook down to a purée, the green lentils retains their shape after cooking.

**1** Melt the butter or margarine in a heavy-bottomed saucepan. Add the bacon, garlic and onion and cook over a moderate to high heat for 5 minutes, stirring constantly.

**2** Lower the heat and add the lentils, celery, carrot, parsley, thyme and bay leaf to the pan. Pour in the stock and 900 ml/1½ pints water. Bring the mixture to the boil, skimming off the scum as it rises to the surface. Add the lemon slice.

**3** Lower the heat, cover the saucepan and then simmer, for 55–60 minutes, stirring occasionally. If the soup is too thick stir in a little water. Carefully remove and discard the sprigs of thyme and parsley, the bay leaf and the lemon slice.

**4** Measure 600 ml/1 pint of the soup mixture and purée it in a blender or food processor until smooth. Return the purée to the soup, stir well and cook over a moderate heat for a further 5 minutes. Serve in heated soup bowls or plates.

*25 g/1 oz butter or margarine*

*125 g/4 oz rindless smoked lean bacon, chopped finely*

*1 garlic clove, chopped finely*

*1 onion, chopped finely*

*425 g/14 oz green lentils, washed, drained and picked over*

*1 celery stick, sliced*

*1 large carrot, diced*

*1 sprig of parsley*

*1 sprig of thyme, or ¼ teaspoon dried thyme*

*1 bay leaf*

*1.2 litres/2 pints Chicken Stock (see page 122)*

*1 slice of lemon*

*salt and pepper*

- Serves 6–8
- Preparation time: 15–20 minutes
- Cooking time: 1¼ hours

# Cauliflower and Cheddar Cheese Soup

**1** Slice the white parts of the spring onions. Finely chop the green parts and set aside.

**2** Melt the butter or margarine in a saucepan and cook the white spring onion parts over a low heat until softened. Add the cauliflower florets and stock. Bring the mixture to the boil, lower the heat and simmer, covered, for 12–15 minutes, or until the cauliflower is tender. Stir in the cheese, the pepper, the mustard and the Worcestershire sauce, with salt to taste. Cook the mixture, uncovered, over a moderate heat until the cheese has melted, stirring constantly.

**3** In a blender or food processor purée the mixture in batches, transferring each successive batch to a clean saucepan.

**4** Add the green parts of the spring onions to the soup. Heat gently over a moderate heat, stirring constantly. Serve the soup in heated soup bowls.

*4 spring onions*

*25 g/1 oz butter or margarine*

*500 g/1 lb cauliflower florets*

*1.2 litres/2 pints Chicken or Vegetable Stock (see page 122)*

*125 g/4 oz mature Cheddar cheese, grated*

*¼ teaspoon white pepper*

*¼ teaspoon prepared English mustard*

*1 teaspoon Worcestershire sauce*

*salt*

- Serves 4–6
- Preparation time: 10 minutes
- Cooking time: about 25 minutes

**96**

# Turkey and Vegetable Soup

**1** Place the drumstick in a large heavy-bottomed saucepan. Add 2.4 litres/4 pints water, the studded onion, parsley sprigs, bouquet garni, salt, thyme and marjoram. Bring the mixture to the boil, lower the heat and simmer, partially covered, for 45 minutes.

**2** Add the chopped onion, carrots and celery. Cook for 30 minutes over a low to moderate heat, then add the lentils, potatoes, leeks and turnips. Cook, until all the vegetables are tender. Remove the drumstick and let it cool. Remove and discard the bouquet garni, the studded onion with cloves and any parsley, thyme or marjoram stems.

**3** Cut the turkey meat off the bone, discarding the skin. Carefully remove any small bones. Cut the meat into small pieces and return it to the saucepan. Add the soy sauce to the pan with pepper to taste. Heat the soup thoroughly and serve in a soup tureen, garnished with the parsley.

- Serves 8
- Preparation time: 25 minutes
- Cooking time: about 2 hours

*1 large turkey drumstick, about 750 g/1½ lb*

*1 small unpeeled onion, studded with 4 cloves plus 1 large onion, peeled and chopped*

*2 sprigs of parsley*

*1 bouquet garni*

*1 teaspoon salt*

*1 sprig of thyme, or ¼ teaspoon dried thyme*

*1 sprig of marjoram, or ½ teaspoon dried marjoram*

*3 carrots, chopped*

*2 celery sticks, sliced*

*250 g/8 oz red lentils washed, drained and picked over*

*250 g/8 oz potatoes, peeled and cut into 1 cm/½ inch cubes*

*3 leeks, trimmed cleaned and sliced*

*3 turnips, peeled and cut into 1 cm/½ inch cubes*

*2 tablespoons light soy sauce*

*pepper*

*3–4 tablespoons finely chopped fresh parsley, to garnish*

# Pot-au-Feu

Pot-au-feu is often referred to as the national soup of France. Although the French treat it as a main course and usually serve the meat separately, there are no firm rules in preparing this substantial dish. In this recipe the pot-au-feu is more of a soup than a main course.

**1** Place the meat and bones in a large saucepan and add cold water to cover. Add the salt and bring the liquid to the boil, skimming off the scum as it rises to the surface.

**2** Lower the heat and add the bouquet garni, peppercorns, studded onion and garlic. Simmer, partially covered, for about 2½ hours, or until the meat is almost tender. Skim from time to time if necessary. Check occasionally if the water level in the saucepan reduces and add more water.

**3** Remove and discard the bones, bouquet garni and studded onion. Add the vegetables and continue to simmer for 1 hour more, or until all the vegetables are tender. Remove the meat, cut it into chunks, then return it to the soup. Serve the soup in large heated soup plates. Sprinkle with plenty of chopped parsley, to garnish.

- Serves 4–6
- Preparation time: 15 minutes
- Cooking time: 3½–4 hours

*1 kg/2 lb clod or shin of beef with bones, excess fat removed*

*1 teaspoon salt*

*1 bouquet garni*

*6 black peppercorns, crushed*

*1 unpeeled onion stuck with 4 cloves*

*1 garlic clove, crushed*

*3 carrots, chopped*

*2 celery sticks, sliced*

*3 leeks, trimmed, cleaned and sliced*

*500 g/1 lb potatoes, peeled and diced*

*3 tablespoons finely chopped fresh parsley, to garnish*

**97**

# Potato and Bacon Soup

This delicious filling soup is illustrated opposite.

**1** Cut the rinds off the bacon and set them aside. Chop the bacon rashers coarsely.

**2** Heat the oil in a heavy-bottomed saucepan and cook the bacon rinds over a moderate heat until crisp, then remove them with a slotted spoon. Discard the rinds.

**3** Add the chopped bacon, onion and garlic to the fat remaining in the pan and cook over a moderate heat for 8–10 minutes or until the onion is light brown and the bacon is fairly crisp. Stir frequently.

**4** Add the stock, 1.2 litres/2 pints water, potatoes, leeks, marjoram, nutmeg and Worcestershire sauce to the pan, with pepper to taste. Bring the mixture to the boil, lower the heat and simmer, covered, for 25 minutes. Stir from time to time.

**5** Blend 600 ml/1 pint of the soup mixture in a blender or food processor for about 2 seconds. Return the coarsely blended mixture to the saucepan. Stir well and cook the soup for a further 10 minutes over a low heat. Add salt to taste. Just before serving stir in the parsley, if using. Serve in heated soup bowls or plates.

*175 g/6 oz smoked bacon rashers with rinds on*

*1 tablespoon olive oil*

*1 onion, chopped finely*

*2 garlic cloves, chopped finely*

*600 ml/1 pint Chicken Stock (see page 122)*

*750 g/1½ lb potatoes, peeled and diced*

*3 leeks, trimmed, cleaned and sliced*

*1 teaspoon chopped fresh, or ½ teaspoon dried marjoram*

*¼ teaspoon ground nutmeg*

*1 teaspoon Worcestershire sauce*

*salt and black pepper*

*3–4 tablespoons finely chopped parsley (optional)*

- Serves 8
- Preparation time: about 20 minutes
- Cooking time: 1 hour

# Harira

A thick Moroccan soup, wholesome and rich in flavour.

**1** Drain the chickpeas in a colander, rinse under cold running water and drain again. Place the chickpeas in a saucepan, cover with 5 cm/2 inches of water and bring to the boil. Lower the heat and simmer, partially covered, for 2 hours, or until tender, adding more water as necessary. Drain the chickpeas and set aside.

**2** Combine the chicken breasts, stock and 1.2 litres/2 pints water in a second saucepan. Bring to the boil, lower the heat, cover the pan and simmer for 10–15 minutes or until the chicken is just cooked. Remove the chicken from the stock, place it on a board and shred it, discarding the skin and any bones. Set the chicken aside.

**3** Add the chickpeas, tomatoes, saffron, onions, rice and lentils to the stock remaining in the pan. Simmer, covered, for 30–35 minutes, or until the rice and lentils are tender.

**4** Just before serving add the shredded chicken, coriander and parsley. Heat the soup for a further 5 minutes without allowing it to boil. Season with salt and pepper.

*250 g/8 oz chickpeas, soaked for 48 hours in cold water to cover or 12 hours if covered in boiling water*

*2 chicken breasts, halved*

*1.2 litres/2 pints Chicken Stock (see page 122)*

*2 x 397 g/14 oz each cans chopped tomatoes*

*¼ teaspoon crumbled saffron strands*

*2 onions, chopped*

*125 g/4 oz long-grain white rice*

*50 g/2 oz green lentils*

*2 tablespoons finely chopped fresh coriander*

*2 tablespoons finely chopped fresh parsley*

*salt and pepper*

- Serves 8–10
- Preparation time: about 25 minutes, plus 12–48 hours soaking
- Cooking time: about 3¼ hours

# Gruyère Soup with Bacon and Potatoes

**1** Heat the oil in a heavy-bottomed saucepan and cook the bacon and onions over a moderate heat until the onion is pale golden. Add the stock, 600 ml/1 pint of 900 ml/1½ pints water and the potatoes. Bring the mixture to the boil, then lower the heat, cover the pan and simmer, for 15 minutes or until the potatoes are tender.

**2** In a small bowl whisk the flour with the remaining 300 ml/½ pint water and stir it into the soup. Cook covered, for 5 minutes, stirring frequently.

**3** In a blender or food processor blend the Gruyère cheese with 300 ml/½ pint of the soup. Stir the purée back into the soup, then add the sherry and Worcestershire sauce with black pepper to taste. Simmer for 3–5 minutes. Serve at once or cool, cover and place in the refrigerator for up to 3 days. Heat thoroughly before serving, stirring in the parsley at the last moment.

*2 tablespoons olive oil*

*3 rashers of rindless smoked bacon, chopped*

*2 onions, chopped finely*

*600 ml/1 pint Chicken Stock (see page 122)*

*625 g/1¼ lb potatoes, peeled and cut into 1 cm/½ inch cubes*

*4 tablespoons plain flour*

*50 g/2 oz grated Gruyère cheese, grated*

*1 tablespoon medium dry sherry*

*1 teaspoon Worcestershire sauce*

*salt and black pepper*

*3 tablespoons finely chopped parsley*

- Serves 6–8
- Preparation time: 20 minutes
- Cooking time: about 25 minutes

# Minestrone

Minestrone is a thick, heavy Italian peasant soup which often provides the whole meal. The variations of this recipe are numerous, but the basis should always be a mixture of beans and fresh vegetables.

**1** Drain the haricot beans in a colander thoroughly, then rinse under cold running water and drain again.

**2** Heat the olive oil in a large saucepan. Add the onions, garlic and bacon. Cook the mixture over a moderate heat until the onions are soft but not brown and the bacon is crisp.

**3** Stir in the tomatoes, 1.8 litres/3 pints water and the beef stock, then add the rinsed beans, the marjoram, thyme and the tomato purée. Bring the mixture to the boil, skimming off the froth as it rises to the surface. Lower the heat and then simmer, covered, for about 2 hours or until the beans are tender.

*250 g/8 oz dried haricot beans, soaked overnight in water to cover*

*3 tablespoons olive oil*

*2 onions, chopped finely*

*2 garlic cloves, chopped finely*

*2 rindless rashers of streaky bacon, chopped finely*

*6 tomatoes, skinned (see page 9) and chopped*

*600 ml/1 pint Beef Stock (see page 120)*

*1 tablespoon chopped fresh marjoram, or 1 teaspoon dried marjoram*

*1 teaspoon chopped fresh thyme, or ½ teaspoon dried thyme*

*2 tablespoons tomato purée*

*2 carrots, diced*

*2 celery sticks, sliced finely*

*½ Savoy cabbage, shredded finely*

*250 g/8 oz fresh shelled or frozen peas*

*50 g/2 oz small pasta shapes*

*1 tablespoon chopped fresh parsley*

*150 g/5 oz grated Parmesan cheese*

*salt and pepper*

**4** Add the carrots and celery and cook over a moderate heat for a further 15 minutes, then add the cabbage, peas and the pasta. Cook for 15–18 minutes or until the vegetables and pasta are tender.

**5** Add a little more water if the soup is too thick. Add the parsley, season with salt and pepper and stir in 50 g/2 oz of the Parmesan. Serve the soup immediately in heated bowls, with the remaining Parmesan served separately.

- Serves 8–10
- Preparation time: about 30 minutes, plus overnight soaking
- Cooking time: about 2¾ hours

# Quick and Easy Soups

Many homemade soups can be cooked in the minimum of time if you make use of some ready-prepared storecupboard ingredients such as canned beans and pulses and tomatoes. A blender or food processor also means that you can achieve a beautifully smooth texture within a very short time and with minimum fuss.

# Avgolemono

There are several ways of preparing this delicious egg and lemon soup from Greece, illustrated on pages 102-3. This is a simple and effective version.

**1** Combine the stock, ½ teaspoon of salt and rice in a saucepan. Bring the mixture to the boil. Stir, lower the heat, cover the pan and simmer for 20 minutes. Stir once more.
**2** Beat the eggs in a small bowl, then whisk in the lemon juice. Add a ladleful of stock, beat, and then add another ladleful of stock and beat again.
**3** Bring the remaining stock and rice mixture to the boil. Briefly remove the saucepan from the heat and add the egg and lemon mixture. Stir well, lower the heat and simmer for a further 2 minutes, add salt and pepper to taste. Sprinkle in the parsley, if liked. Serve immediately in heated bowls.

*1.5 litres/2½ pints Chicken Stock (see page 122)*
*50 g/2 oz long-grain white rice*
*2 eggs*
*2-3 tablespoons lemon juice*
*salt and pepper*
*1 tablespoon chopped fresh parsley (optional)*

- Serves 4–6
- Preparation time: about 10 minutes
- Cooking time: 25 minutes

# Tomato Chowder

**1** Combine all the ingredients except the cheese in a large saucepan. Stir well. Bring to the boil over a moderate heat, stirring all the time, then lower the heat and simmer, uncovered, for 3 minutes.
**2** Ladle the soup into heated ovenproof bowls, sprinkle with the cheese and place under a preheated hot grill for 3–5 minutes, until the cheese is bubbling. Serve immediately.

*1 x 300 g/10 oz can condensed tomato soup*
*1 x 397 g/14 oz can tomatoes, sieved*
*1 x 325 g/11 oz can sweetcorn, drained*
*1 tablespoon Worcestershire sauce*
*3-6 drops of Tabasco sauce*
*1 teaspoon chopped fresh oregano or ½ teaspoon dried oregano*
*½ teaspoon sugar*
*125 g/4 oz Cheddar cheese, grated*

- Serves 4–6
- Preparation time: 5 minutes
- Cooking time: about 10 minutes

# Tomato and Lemon Broth with Oregano

**1** Drain the canned tomatoes, reserving half the juice in a jug. Melt the butter or margarine in a saucepan and cook the tomatoes for 5 minutes over a moderate heat, stirring and breaking them up with a wooden spoon.

**2** Add the reserved tomato juice, stock, lemon juice and rind with plenty of ground black pepper to taste. Stir in the sugar, Tabasco sauce and Worcestershire sauce. Bring the liquid to the boil, then lower the heat and simmer, uncovered, for 15 minutes.

**3** Stir in the oregano and parsley and simmer the soup for a further 5 minutes. Remove the soup from the heat and rub it through a fine sieve into a clean saucepan. Heat briefly if necessary. Divide the soup between 4 heated bowls and garnish each portion with a lemon slice.

*1 x 397 g/14 oz can plum tomatoes*

*25 g/1 oz butter or margarine*

*600 ml/1 pint Chicken or Vegetable Stock (see page 122)*

*2 tablespoons lemon juice*

*1 teaspoon grated lemon rind*

*freshly ground black pepper*

*½ teaspoon sugar*

*4 drops of Tabasco sauce, or to taste*

*2 teaspoons Worcestershire sauce*

*1 tablespoon chopped fresh oregano, or 1 teaspoon dried oregano*

*1 tablespoon chopped fresh parsley*

*4 thin lemon slices*

- Serves 4
- Preparation time: 5–8 minutes
- Cooking time: 25 minutes

# Beetroot Sorbet

A cooling, mouthwatering starter that needs little preparation and no cooking.

**1** Chop the beetroot roughly and place it in a blender or food processor. Add the wine and peppercorns, with salt to taste. Purée until very smooth, then pour the mixture into a shallow freezerproof dish. Freeze the mixture for 1–2 hours, or until ice crystals from around the edges. Stir with a fork to break up the ice crystals, then return the mixture to the freezer until solid.

**2** Line 4 chilled glasses or glass bowls with lettuce leaves and fill them with scoops of the sorbet. Top each portion with a teaspoon of soured cream sprinkled with chives or spring onion tops. Serve at once.

*325 g/11 oz peeled cooked beetroot*

*150 ml/¼ pint dry white wine*

*1 teaspoon green peppercorns*

*salt*

*To garnish:*

*crisp lettuce leaves*

*4 tablespoons soured cream*

*snipped fresh chives or finely chopped spring onion tops*

- Serves 4
- Preparation time: 5 minutes, plus 2–3 hours freezing time

# Crab meat Bisque

This delicious soup, illustrated opposite, is one of my favourites. It takes only minutes to make, yet tastes as though a great deal of effort has gone into its preparation.

**1** Combine the tomato soup and milk in a saucepan. Stir well over a moderate to high heat for 3 minutes. Add the crab meat with the brine, then stir in the curry powder, Worcestershire sauce and sherry. Cook for a further 3 minutes, or until the soup is almost boiling.

**2** Remove the saucepan from the heat and stir in the cream. Serve the soup in heated soup bowls. Garnish each portion with snipped fresh chives or finely chopped parsley, if using . If the bisque is intended to be more substantial, serve with croûtons (see page 66).

*1 x 300 g/10 oz can condensed tomato soup*

*300 ml/½ pint milk*

*1 x 175 g/6 oz can white crab meat in brine*

*½ teaspoon mild curry powder*

*1 teaspoon Worcestershire sauce*

*2 teaspoons medium dry sherry*

*2 tablespoons double cream*

*snipped fresh chives or finely chopped fresh parsley, to garnish (optional)*

- Serves 3–4
- Preparation time: 3–5 minutes
- Cooking time: about 6 minutes

# Simple Cabbage Soup

**1** Heat the butter and oil in a saucepan. Add the onion and garlic and cook, stirring frequently, for 5 minutes.

**2** Add the cabbage, potatoes and stock to the pan with salt and pepper to taste. Bring the mixture to the boil. Lower the heat, cover the saucepan and simmer the soup, covered, for about 45 minutes.

**3** Serve at once in heated soup plates or bowls. Garnish each portion with crumbled bacon.

*50 g/2 oz butter*

*1 tablespoon olive oil*

*2 onions, sliced finely*

*1 garlic clove, crushed*

*½ small green cabbage, shredded finely*

*2 potatoes, peeled and sliced thinly*

*750 ml/1¼ pints Beef Stock (see page 120)*

*salt and pepper*

*2 rashers streaky bacon, fried until crisp, crumbled, to garnish*

- Serves 4–6
- Preparation time: 10 minutes
- Cooking time: about 50 minutes

# Chinese Cabbage Soup

A simple soup with a distinctly Oriental flavour.

**1** Heat the olive oil in a large saucepan over a low heat, add the crushed garlic and cook for 1 minute, stirring constantly.

**2** Add the Chinese cabbage, stock and soy sauce to the pan. Bring to the boil, then lower the heat, cover the pan and simmer the mixture for 3–5 minutes, or until the cabbage is tender. Add salt and pepper to taste. Serve at once, in heated bowls.

*1½ tablespoons olive oil*

*1 garlic clove, crushed*

*250 g/8 oz Chinese cabbage, leaves and stalks chopped*

*600 ml/1 pint Chicken Stock (see page 122)*

*1 tablespoon light soy sauce*

*salt and pepper*

- Serves 2
- Preparation time: 5 minutes
- Cooking time: 5–7 minutes

# Chinese Sweetcorn Soup with Crab Meat

**1** Whisk the egg white with the sesame oil in a small bowl. Set aside. In a separate bowl mix the cornflour to a paste with 2 teaspoons of water.

**2** Bring the stock to the boil in a saucepan. Add the sweetcorn and cook for 10 minutes over a moderate heat. Then add the sherry, ginger, salt and sugar and stir in the cornflour mixture. Bring to the boil, lower the heat and simmer for 3-5 minutes, stirring frequently.

**3** Add the crab meat to the pan and stir well. Cook for 2 minutes. Pour in the reserved egg white mixture slowly and in a steady stream, stirring constantly. Ladle the soup into a warmed tureen and sprinkle with the green spring onion tops, to garnish. Serve at once.

*1 egg white*

*1 teaspoon sesame oil*

*2 teaspoons cornflour*

*2 teaspoons water*

*1.2 litres/2 pints Chicken Stock (see page 122)*

*275 g/9 oz drained canned or thawed frozen sweetcorn*

*2 tablespoons dry sherry*

*2 teaspoons grated fresh root ginger*

*½ teaspoon salt*

*1 teaspoon sugar*

*1 x 175 g/6 oz can white crab meat in brine, drained*

*2 tablespoons finely chopped spring onion tops, to garnish*

- Serves 4–6
- Preparation time: 12–15 minutes
- Cooking time: about 15–18 minutes

# Oriental Bean sprout and Mooli Soup

**1** Cut the mooli in half, then in quarters lengthways. Chop it into 1 cm/½ inch dice.

**2** Combine the beef stock and diced mooli in a large pan. Bring the stock to the boil, then lower the heat and simmer, uncovered, for about 15 minutes. The mooli should be almost translucent.

**3** Cut the spring onions tops into 5 cm/2 inches lengths; cut each bulb in half or quarters, depending on thickness. Add to the pan with the bean sprouts and soy sauce. Season with black pepper and cook over a moderate heat for a further 5-8 minutes. Serve at once in heated bowls.

*250 g/8 oz mooli, peeled*

*1.2 litres/2 pints Beef Stock (see page 120)*

*5 spring onions*

*200 g/7 oz fresh bean sprouts, washed and drained*

*2 tablespoons dark soy sauce*

*black pepper to taste*

- Serves 4
- Preparation time: 10 minutes
- Cooking time: about 20 minutes

**109**

# Cream of Celery and Prawn Soup

This fragrant, smooth soup, illustrated opposite, may be served hot or chilled and takes only minutes to prepare.

**1** Mix the can of celery soup and the milk in a saucepan. Add the paprika and white pepper. Bring to a simmering point, stirring constantly for 5 minutes. Take the pan off the heat.
**2** If serving the soup hot, stir in the yogurt and prawns and reheat gently for about 2 minutes. Do not boil. Serve in heated bowls, garnishing each portion with snipped chives.
**3** If serving the soup chilled, pour the soup into a bowl and leave to cool. Stir in the yogurt and prawns, cover the bowl and chill for at least 3 hours. Serve the soup in chilled bowls, garnishing each portion with snipped chives.

*1 x 300 g/10 oz can condensed cream of celery soup*

*300 ml/½ pint milk*

*1 teaspoon paprika*

*½ teaspoon white pepper*

*2 tablespoons natural yogurt*

*150 g/5 oz cooked peeled prawns thoroughly defrosted if frozen*

*snipped fresh chives, to garnish*

- Serves 2–3
- Preparation time: 3-5 minutes, plus 3 hours chilling time
- Cooking time, if serving cold: 5 minutes

# Spinach Soup

Although frozen leaf spinach can be used for this recipe, the full-flavoured taste of fresh spinach cannot be matched.

**1** Melt the butter or margarine in a heavy-bottomed saucepan. Add the onion and cook over a moderate heat until soft but not golden. Add the spinach and cook until soft, stirring constantly.

**2** Pour the chicken or vegetable stock into the pan and add the potatoes, lemon juice and nutmeg with salt and pepper to taste. Cook, partially covered, over a moderate heat for 10–12 minutes, or until the potatoes are soft.

**3** In a blender or food processor purée the mixture in batches until smooth, transferring each successive batch to a clean saucepan. Add the cream and heat the soup gently without boiling. Serve in heated soup bowls, sprinkling each portion with ground almonds, to garnish, if liked.

*50 g/2 oz butter or margarine*

*1 onion, chopped*

*500 g/1 lb fresh or frozen spinach*

*1.2 litres/2 pints Chicken or Vegetable Stock (see page 122)*

*250 g/8 oz potatoes, peeled and thinly sliced*

*1 teaspoon lemon juice*

*pinch of grated nutmeg*

*150 ml/¼ pint double cream*

*salt and white pepper*

*ground almonds, to garnish (optional)*

- Serves 4–6
- Preparation time: 10 minutes
- Cooking time: about 20 minutes

## Variation

# Chilled Spinach Soup

Follow the main recipe but omit the double cream and ground almonds. Pour the puréed soup into a bowl, cover and chill for at least 3 hours in the refrigerator. In a small bowl blend 150 ml/¼ pint soured cream with 1 teaspoon finely grated onion and 2 tablespoons peeled and diced cucumber. Serve the soup in chilled bowls, topping each portion with a little of the soured cream mixture.

- Serves 4–6
- Preparation time: 10 minutes, plus 3 hours chilling time
- Cooking time: about 20 minutes

# Chickpea and Watercress Soup

**1** Melt the butter or margarine in a large saucepan. Add the onion and garlic and cook until the onion is beginning to soften but has not changed colour.

**2** Add the lentils and the rice to the onion and garlic mixture. Stir and pour in the stock. Bring to the boil, then lower the heat, cover the pan and simmer for 15-18 minutes, or until the lentils and rice are tender.

**3** Add the watercress and chickpeas. Simmer the soup for a further 8–10 minutes. Season with salt and pepper and serve in heated bowls.

*550 g/2 oz butter or margarine*

*1 onion, chopped*

*1 garlic clove, crushed*

*50 g/2 oz red lentils, washed, drained and picked over*

*50 g/2 oz long-grain white rice*

*1.8 litres/3 pints Chicken or Vegetable Stock (see page 122)*

*1 bunch watercress, thick stems discarded, rinsed, drained and chopped roughly*

*1 x 425 g/14 oz can chick-peas, drained*

*salt and pepper*

- Serves 4–6
- Preparation time: 5–8 minutes
- Cooking time: about 30 minutes

# Orange Consommé

A deliciously refreshing starter to any meal. The preparation takes hardly any time at all, and if you want to speed up the chilling process, cool and cover the consommé then place it in the freezer until the surface is covered with a thin layer of ice.

**1** Pour the consommé into a pan. Squeeze the juice from the oranges and add to the pan with the cloves and cayenne to taste. Bring the mixture to the boil, then remove the cloves, using a slotted spoon. Tip the contents of the pan into a bowl and set aside.

**2** When the orange consommé is cool, cover the surface closely and chill for 3–4 hours in the refrigerator. Alternatively freeze the mixture for about 30 minutes, until the surface is covered with a thin layer of ice.

**3** Serve in chilled bowls, garnishing each portion with an orange slice.

*1 x 475 g/15 oz can beef consommé*

*3 oranges*

*2 cloves*

*cayenne pepper, to taste*

*1 orange, sliced thinly, to garnish*

- Serves 6
- Preparation time: 3-5 minutes, plus 3–4 hours chilling time
- Cooking time: 3–5 minutes

# Lentil and Tomato Soup

This quick and tasty soup is illustrated opposite.

**1** Drain the canned tomatoes, reserving the juice in a jug or bowl. Chop the tomatoes roughly and set aside.

**2** Melt the butter or margarine in a saucepan and add the onion and bacon. Cook, over a low heat until the onion is soft and golden. Stir in the lentils, stock, chopped tomatoes and reserved tomato juice. Bring the mixture to the boil, stirring occasionally. Lower the heat, cover the pan and simmer the mixture for 15 minutes or until the lentils are soft.

**3** In a blender or food processor purée the soup in batches until smooth, transferring each successive batch to a clean saucepan. Add salt and pepper to taste. Heat the soup gently. Serve at once, in heated soup plates or bowls, garnishing each portion with a swirl of cream and a sprinkling of chives or parsley.

*1 x 397 g/14 oz can plum tomatoes*

*50 g/2 oz butter or margarine*

*1 large onion, chopped*

*2 rashers of rindless smoked back bacon, chopped finely*

*125 g/4 oz red lentils, rinsed*

*600 ml/1 pint Chicken Stock (see page 122)*

*salt and pepper*

*To garnish:*

*2 tablespoons double cream*

*snipped fresh chives or finely chopped fresh parsley*

- Serves 4
- Preparation time: 10 minutes
- Cooking time: about 20 minutes

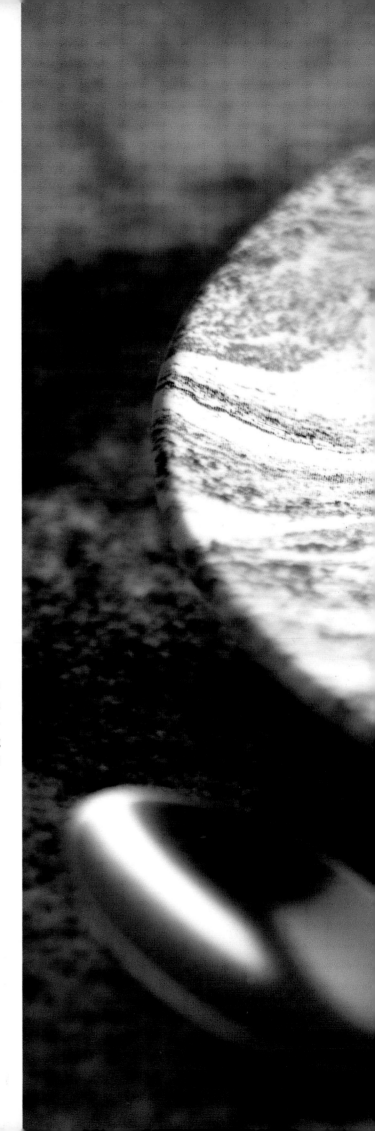

# Pea and Mint Soup

1 Melt the butter or margarine in a saucepan, add the onion and cook over a moderate heat until soft but not golden. Stir frequently.

2 Add the peas, the sugar, stock and 3 tablespoons of the chopped mint. Stir in white pepper to taste and bring the mixture to the boil. Add the potatoes, lower the heat and simmer, partially covered, for 20–25 minutes.

3 In a blender or food processor purée the mixture in batches until smooth, transferring each successive batch to a clean saucepan. Season with salt, add the cream and stir well. Heat the soup gently without boiling. Serve in heated soup plates or bowls. Garnish with the remaining chopped mint.

**50 g/2 oz butter or margarine**

**1 small onion, chopped**

**500 g/1 lb frozen green peas**

**¼ teaspoon sugar**

**1.2 litres/2 pints Chicken or Vegetable Stock (see page 122)**

**4 tablespoons chopped fresh mint**

**300 g/10 oz potatoes, peeled and coarsely chopped**

**150 ml/¼ pint double cream**

**salt and white pepper**

- Serves 6
- Preparation time: 5–10 minutes
- Cooking time: 30–35 minutes

## Variation

# Chilled Pea Soup with Mint

Make the soup as described in the main recipe, but transfer it to a bowl, not a saucepan, after puréeing. Do not add the cream at this stage. Instead, allow the soup to cool, then cover closely and chill for at least 3 hours. Chill the cream. Just before serving, swirl in the chilled cream. Serve in chilled bowls, garnishing each portion with mint.

- Serves 6
- Preparation time: 5–10 minutes, plus 3 hours chilling time
- Cooking time: 30-35 minutes

**116**

# Jellied Consommé with Curry Cream

1 Pour the consommé into a saucepan and sprinkle the gelatine on top. Heat gently until the gelatine has dissolved. Remove the saucepan from the heat, cool slightly, then stir in the sherry. Leave to cool.

2 Pour the consommé into 4 ramekin dishes and place them in the refrigerator to set.

3 In a bowl mix the curry powder with ½ tablespoon of boiling water. Blend in the cream and whisk until it thickens.

4 Unmould the set consommé by dipping the base of each ramekin dish into very hot water for a second; then invert the jellied consommé on to a plate. Spoon the curry cream over the top so that it begins to trickle down the sides. Garnish each serving with a teaspoon of lumpfish (optional) and a sprinkling of chives or dill. Serve immediately.

*1x 475 g/15 oz can beef consommé*

*1 teaspoon gelatine powder*

*3 tablespoons dry sherry*

*½ tablespoon mild curry powder*

*8 tablespoons double cream*

*To garnish:*

*4 teaspoons lumpfish (optional)*

*1 tablespoon fresh snipped chives or dill*

- Serves 4
- Preparation time: 10 minutes, plus 1 hour chilling time
- Cooking time: 1 hour

# Speedy Soup

This is an easy, convenient way to use up leftover meat or poultry from Sunday's roast or the Christmas turkey. Vary the vegetables accordingly to availablilty – parsnip, turnips and shredded cabbage leaves may be added.

1 Melt the butter or margarine in a large saucepan. Add the onion, garlic and celery, cover the pan and cook over a moderate heat for 5 minutes, or until the vegetables begin to soften.

2 Add the stock, potatoes, carrots and leeks. Bring to the boil, lower the heat and simmer, partially covered, for 25 minutes or until all the vegetable are tender but not too soft. Add the meat and cook for 5 minutes more. Stir in the parsley. Serve at once in heated soup plates or bowls.

*50 g/2 oz butter or margarine*

*1 onion, chopped finely*

*1 garlic clove, crushed*

*1 celery stick, sliced*

*1.2 litres/2 pints Chicken Stock (see page 122)*

*500 g/1 lb potatoes, peeled and cut into small cubes*

*250 g/8 oz carrots, chopped*

*2 leeks trimmed, cleaned and sliced*

*250–325 g/8–11 oz cooked chicken, goose, duck or turkey meat, shredded*

*2 tablespoons finely chopped parsley*

- Serves 6
- Preparation time: 10-–5 minutes
- Cooking time: 35 minutes

**117**

# Basic Stocks

This chapter contains the basic recipes that are essential to many of the recipes within this book. Although commercially made stock cubes or bought ready-made stock can be used, a good homemade stock gives an excellent foundation to a soup. All these stocks will keep for 2–3 days in the refrigerator or between 2–4 months in the freezer. (See individual recipes for exact timings.)

# Basic Beef Stock

A rich stock is an excellent foundation for many meat and vegetable soups. Ask the butcher to chop the bones into manageable pieces.

**1** Place the bones in a large saucepan. Cover them with 3.4 litres/6 pints water and add the salt. Bring the liquid to the boil, skimming off any scum that rises to the surface. Lower the heat, cover the pan partially and simmer over a low heat for 2 hours. Skim from time to time with a slotted spoon.

*about 1 kg/2 lb marrow and shin bones*

*1 teaspoon salt*

*1 onion, quartered*

*2 celery sticks, chopped coarsely with the leaves*

*2 carrots, coarsely chopped*

*4 parsley sprigs*

*1 bouquet garni*

*8 black peppercorns*

**2** Add the remaining ingredients and continue to simmer for a further 2 hours. Add more water if the level drops below that of the bones.

**3** Cool slightly, then strain the stock through a fine sieve into a bowl, discarding the bones, vegetables, herbs and spices. Leave the stock to cool. Skim off the fat with a spoon or blot with kitchen paper. Cover the stock and refrigerate it. Use within 3 days. This stock is suitable for freezing; if frozen use within 3 months.

- Makes 3.4 litres/6 pints
- Preparation time: 15 minutes
- Cooking time: about 4 hours

## Variation

# Dark Beef Stock

Place the bones in a roasting tin, spreading them out in a single layer. Cook in a preheated oven 230°C (425°F), Gas Mark 7, for about 20 minutes (less if the bones have been roasted before). Meanwhile fry the vegetables in 1 tablespoon of oil, lard or dripping until well browned. Transfer the bones to a large saucepan, add the water and salt and proceed as in the main recipe, adding the drained browned vegetables with the spices.

- Makes 3.4 litres/6 pints
- Preparation time: 15 minutes
- Cooking time: about 4½ hours

# Fish Stock

The heads, tails and bones of white fish, such as cod, haddock, plaice, hake or whiting make a good stock, but oily fish like mackerel and herring are not suitable.

**1** Place the fish trimmings in a large saucepan and cover with 900 ml/1½ pints water. Add all the remaining ingredients, stir well and bring to the boil, skimming off the froth as it rises to the surface. Lower the heat and simmer, partially covered, for 30–40 minutes.

**2** Remove the saucepan from the heat and strain the mixture through a sieve, discarding the fish trimmings and other ingredients. Cool, then cover closely and chill in the refrigerator. Use within 2 days. This stock is suitable for freezing; if frozen use within 2 months.

*500 g/1 lb fish trimmings (bones, heads, tails, skins)*

*1 onion, quartered*

*1 celery stick with leaves, chopped coarsely*

*1 bay leaf*

*1 sprig of parsley*

*¼ teaspoon salt*

*6 black peppercorns*

*150 ml/¼ pint dry white wine or cider*

- Makes about 1 litre/1¾ pints
- Preparation time: 5–8 minutes
- Cooking time: 40 minutes

## Variation

# White Fish Stock

This makes an excellent base for chowders and bisque.

**1** Butter a heavy-bottomed saucepan and put in the fish trimmings. Add the onion, parsley, bay leaf, peppercorns, lemon juice and salt. Cover the pan tightly and steam the mixture, over a moderate heat for about 5 minutes.

**2** Add 1 litre/1½ pints water and wine and bring the mixture to the boil, skimming off the froth as it rises to the surface. Cook the stock, covered, over a moderate heat for 45 minutes.

**3** Remove the saucepan from the heat and strain the mixture through a sieve into a bowl, discarding the fish trimmings and other ingredients. Cool, then cover closely and chill in the refrigerator. Use within 2 days. This stock is suitable for freezing; if frozen use within 2 months.

*25 g/1 oz butter*

*500 g/1 lb trimmings from white fish (cod, haddock, plaice, hake, whiting, sole or monkfish)*

*1 onion, quartered*

*3 sprigs of parsley*

*1 bay leaf*

*6 white peppercorns*

*2 tablespoons lemon juice*

*½ teaspoon salt*

*1 litre/1¾ pints water*

*150 ml/¼ pint dry white wine*

- Makes about 1.2 litres/2 pints
- Preparation time: 5–8 minutes
- Cooking time: 50 minutes

121

# Chicken Stock

**1** Put the carcass into a deep saucepan, cover with 3.4 litres/6 pints water and add the salt. Bring to the boil, skimming off the scum with a slotted spoon. Lower the heat, partially cover the pan and simmer for 1 hour.

**2** Add the onion, celery, carrots, parsley, bouquet garni, bay leaf and peppercorns. Stir and continue simmering, partially covered, for a further 1½–2 hours. Add more water if the level drops below the bones.

**3** Cool slightly. Remove the carcass, then strain the stock through a fine sieve into a bowl, discarding all the vegetable and herbs. After straining the stock, pick over the carcass, remove any meat still on the bones and add it to the stock.

**4** Leave to cool, then skim off the fat with a spoon or blot with kitchen paper. Cover the stock, refrigerate it and use within 3 days. This stock is suitable for freezing; if frozen use within 3 months.

- Makes about 3.4 litres/6 pints
- Preparation time: 5–8 minutes
- Cooking time: about 3 hours

*1 whole chicken carcass*

*1 teaspoon salt*

*1 Spanish onion peeled, stuck with 4 cloves*

*2 celery sticks, chopped*

*2 carrots, chopped coarsely*

*2 sprigs of parsley*

*1 bouquet garni*

*1 bay leaf*

*8 black peppercorns*

# Vegetable Stock

A dark vegetable stock can be made by adding 250 g/8 oz chopped flat mushrooms to the vegetable stock with the other vegetables.

**1** Combine 1.8 litres/3 pints water with all the remaining ingredients in a deep saucepan. Bring to the boil, then lower the heat and simmer, covered, for 2½–3 hours. Skim from time to time.

**2** Cool, then strain through a sieve, discarding all the vegetables and herbs in the sieve. Cover the stock closely and store in the refrigerator. Use within 3-4 days. This stock is suitable for freezing; if frozen use within 4 months.

- Makes about 1.8 litres/3 pints
- Preparation time: 15 minutes
- Cooking time: 2½–3 hours

*1 unpeeled onion, halved*

*1 unpeeled garlic clove, halved*

*1 carrot, chopped coarsely*

*1 celery stick with leaves, chopped coarsely*

*¼ small unpeeled swede, coarsely chopped*

*1 leek, white and green parts, chopped coarsely*

*1 sprig of parsley*

*6 black peppercorns*

*1 bay leaf*

*1 bouquet garni*

*salt*

*peelings of 1–2 scrubbed potatoes*

*outer leaves of cauliflower, cabbage, Brussels sprouts (optional)*

# Index

# D

# E